CLAUDE M. BRISTOL'S

THE MAGIC OF BELIEVING

CLAUDE M. BRISTOL'S
THE MAGIC OF BELIEVING

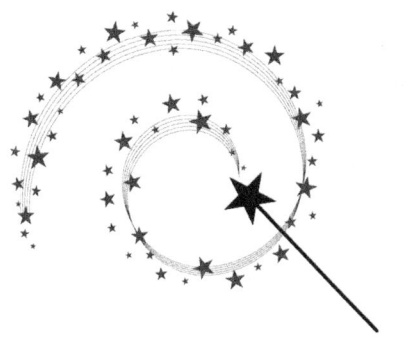

A MODERN-DAY INTERPRETATION
OF A SELF-HELP CLASSIC
BY ANDREW HOLMES

Copyright © Infinite Ideas Limited, 2013

First published in 2013 by

Infinite Ideas Limited
36 St Giles
Oxford
OX1 3LD
United Kingdom
www.infideas.com

All rights reserved. Except for the quotation of small passages for the purposes of criticism or review, no part of this publication may be reproduced, stored in a retrieval system or transmitted in any form or by any means, electronic, mechanical, photocopying, recording, scanning or otherwise, except under the terms of the Copyright, Designs and Patents Act 1988 or under the terms of a licence issued by the Copyright Licensing Agency Ltd, 90 Tottenham Court Road, London W1T 4LP, U.K., without the permission in writing of the publisher. Requests to the publisher should be addressed to the Permissions Department, Infinite Ideas Limited, 36 St Giles, Oxford, OX1 3LD, U.K., or faxed to +44 (0) 1865 514777.

A CIP catalogue record for this book is available from the British Library.

ISBN 978–1–906821–32–6

Brand and product names are trademarks or registered trademarks of their respective owners.

CONTENTS

INTRODUCTION..................................8

1. ACT DECISIVELY 10
2. FOLLOW THAT THOUGHT......................12
3. HOLDING ONTO SUCCESS 14
4. MOULDED BY OTHERS.........................16
5. SLEEP ON IT...................................18
6. THE LIFELINE..................................20
7. THE POWER OF TALISMANS 22
8. TRUMPING INTIMIDATION.....................24
9. YOUR BODY SPEAKS ITS MIND..................26
10. APPEAL BY DRAMA 28
11. CONNECTING THE DOTS 30
12. IF YOU BELIEVE IT, WRITE IT DOWN 32
13. MENTAL MODELS 34
14. SEEK AND YOU SHALL FIND 36
15. THE INNER GAME.............................38
16. THE POWER OF PHYSIOLOGY...................40
17. THINK YOUR WORLD INTO BEING 42
18. WHAT WOULD EDISON SAY?...................44
19. BE UNFLAPPABLE.............................46
20. HARD WORK IS NOT ENOUGH 48

21. THE FOUNDATIONS OF TRUST................... 50
22. THINK THE BEST OF OTHERS 52
23. KNOW YOUR LIMITATIONS..................... 54
24. NO ONE IS AN ISLAND......................... 56
25. BELIEVING OTHERS 58
26. HAVE FAITH 60
27. VISUALIZATION 62
28. THE INVISIBLE HAND.......................... 64
29. YOU ARE WHAT YOU READ 66
30. IT'S NOT WHAT YOU SAY, IT'S 68
    THE WAY THAT YOU SAY IT
31. THE MYSTERIOUS MAGNETISM OF POSITIVITY.... 70
32. REGRETS ... I HAVE A FEW...................... 72
33. THE MIRROR TECHNIQUE....................... 74
34. SCRUPULOUS OPTIMISM....................... 76
35. THINKING BIG TO BE BIG 78
36. BREAKING CONVENTION 80
37. CAN-DO CULTURE 82
38. KNOW THYSELF............................... 84
39. SMILE AND THE WHOLE WORLD................ 86
    SMILES WITH YOU
40. FROM THE FRINGE............................ 88
41. WHAT DO YOU WANT? 90
42. THE CARD TECHNIQUE........................ 92

43. THE POWER OF DESIRE	94
44. HAVING THE COURAGE OF YOUR CONVICTIONS	96
45. ME ... A CHIEF EXECUTIVE?	98
46. TO CONVINCE OTHERS, YOU MUST FIRST CONVINCE YOURSELF	100
47 EVERYTHING CAN BE IMPROVED	102
48 MANTRAS AND SELF-AFFIRMATIONS	104
49 THE PLACEBO EFFECT	106
50 THE WHOLE PACKAGE	108
51 SET THE SCENE FOR SUCCESS	110
52 THE SINGULARITY	112

INTRODUCTION

***The Magic of Believing* was no quick fix, but it was ahead of its time.**

When Claude Bristol wrote *The Magic of Believing*, he did so because he was convinced about the power of thought and suggestion. His idea wasn't just whimsical, nor was it a quick fix; Bristol took the time to think about his concept and research it too. It is this that allows the book to survive the test of time.

The germ of his idea came to him whilst in the trenches of the First World War and although he may have had a gentler ride than most, it was during his time in France, when he had no money, that he decided that he would become rich. His notion of becoming rich was not a fleeting wish or daydream, but something altogether more powerful; it was a decision, a powerful desire. Having made the decision, his mind and all its underlying power was focused on achieving it. Although this took time, he believed that every action (both his and others) helped him to realize his objective. Bristol did indeed become rich.

Bristol researched his ideas carefully and like all good scholars cast his net wide. In addition to doing what most people would do when trying to understand how successful people became successful, he investigated religions, sects and organizations. From this he deduced that with repeated suggestion and mantras, talismans and such like, it was not only possible to make people believe in something, be it their own capabilities or God, but it also allowed them to become masters of their own destiny. The key was believing in the power of thought.

Bristol was clearly ahead of his time and because of this his ideas were often met with scepticism and, occasionally, derision. He acknowledged this but felt that his ideas, and the evidence he accrued to support them, were solid. He was also keen to stress that this was no quick fix. To harness the power of thought required congruence between what people wanted and what they did – it went to the heart of who they were. It therefore necessitated hard work and diligence. This was no ordinary self-help, quick fix, this was something more enduring. Interestingly much later in the century, when the clinical basis for neurolinguistic programming was established, his ideas finally received the credibility they deserved.

In this modern day interpretation of Bristol's book, the key themes and ideas have been distilled into 52 bite-sized chunks, supported by examples from business and sport as well as history and human endeavour. Designed to provide a short-cut to the concepts, this book provides the reader with a solid grounding in *The Magic of Believing* and everything they need to harness the power of the mind, something which Bristol realized back in 1918.

1 ACT DECISIVELY

Bristol rightly recognized procrastination as the thief of time. One of the most important skills you should learn if you want to avoid this thief is that of making decisive decisions because, 'in not deciding you fail to act, and in failing to act you invite failure. Experience will soon teach you that once a decision is made, the problems and troubles begin to disappear. Even though the decision you make may not be the best one, the mere deciding gives you strength and raises your morale.'

'*The Magic of Believing* is not just about the power of thought per se, as even Bristol recognized that there was more to it than that. Throughout the book he poses questions to the reader in order to get them to think about the other factors that, although not central to the ideas associated with suggestion, were still important. One such area was decision making. Bristol believed that the reason why there are so few leaders and so many followers in the world was that too many of us are afraid to make decisions. He quite rightly pointed out that when confronted with a problem, the longer you put it off, the greater it becomes and the more fearful you become of your ability to solve it.

We make myriad decisions every day, some trivial, many automatic, and others more significant. Although we may be good at the routine and trivial decisions, those with more significance attached to them are often harder to make because we have more to lose if they are poor. We agonize over them before we take them and then ruminate when we have. But, as Bristol points out, taking no decision is worse than making a bad one and by taking a decision you have placed a stake in the ground; from this you can determine if it was good or bad and act accordingly. Achieving what you want out of life and your career and, indeed, from the power of thought which Bristol advocates, requires that you act decisively. Over time, this ability gets easier as the combination of your accumulated knowledge and experience allows you to rely on your gut instinct (à la Jack Welch), and something which Malcolm Gladwell, in *Blink*, terms 'thin slicing'. Our subconscious becomes so well-tuned that we know instinctively what course of action to take and what decision to make. For those who have yet to accumulate such a wealth of knowledge and experience, it is always a good idea to remember the three steps to making a decision: the recognition of a need; a decision to change; and a conscious dedication to implementing the decision.

DEFINING IDEA...

'Men make history and not the other way around. In periods where there is no leadership, society stands still. Progress occurs when courageous, skilful leaders seize the opportunity to change things for the better.'

HARRY S. TRUMAN, US PRESIDENT

HERE'S AN IDEA FOR YOU...

The next time you find yourself stuck on a decision, try the following. Instead of worrying about what might happen if you make the decision, recalibrate your decision-making process by thinking about what you might lose if you fail to take it.

2 FOLLOW THAT THOUGHT

'The automobile, the skyscraper, the great planes that sweep the stratosphere, the sewing machine, the tiny pin, a thousand and one things – yes, millions of objects – where did they come from originally? Only one source. From that strange force – thought.' *The Magic of Believing* **requires that we pay attention to and follow our thoughts.**

It is interesting that computer scientists continue to strive to create artificial intelligence even though we have yet to unravel the full mysteries of the brain. Clearly computers are great at processing vast amounts of data, but there is one aspect of the brain that is probably its most powerful asset and one that may never be replicated inside a computer: the capacity for emergent thinking. Bristol makes a few statements that not only capture the essence of what *The Magic of Believing* is all about, but also sums up this superb ability of the brain.

The capacity for unique thought is also accompanied by its very fragility. As Bristol quite rightly points out, 'A passing or momentary thought-flicker dies almost aborning.' To be truly successful therefore, we must be conscious of the emergent properties of our thinking and be alert to what is present. Once a thought pops into our mind we should give it time to grow and develop. In other words we should follow it. There are plenty of examples throughout history of the willingness to do just that. Take Johannes Kepler, who believed the planets moved in elliptical orbits about the sun. His idea was not just (quite literally) revolutionary, as it went against the church's geocentric belief (people were burned at the stake for suggesting otherwise), but it also went against the received wisdom of Ptolemy and Copernicus who believed the orbits were circular in nature. His revolutionary thought came from observation and the belief that the existing theories did not chime with observable reality. To prove the point he slaved away for seven years reviewing observations made by himself and others, such as the astronomer and mathematician Tycho Brahe, until he came up with mathematical theory that explained them. So great was his achievement that NASA still uses his theories to navigate the vast expanse of our solar system and plan such amazing ventures as the Mars landing. All this from one thought ... quite extraordinary.

DEFINING IDEA...

'The diversity of the phenomena of nature is so great, and the treasures hidden in the heavens so rich, precisely in order that the human mind shall never be lacking in fresh nourishment.'

JOHANNES KEPLER, ASTRONOMER

HERE'S AN IDEA FOR YOU...

One of the most effective ways to follow a thought is to capture it as it enters your head. Rather than just let it die, why not jot it down? Keep a notepad on you at all times and by your bed at night so that when an idea comes to you, you can write it down. You can then review it at your leisure and see if it is worth following.

3 HOLDING ONTO SUCCESS

'Success is a matter of never-ceasing application. You must forever work at it. At no time can you afford to rest on your laurels – a pause for self-admiration – because there are others who may have eyes on your coveted place and who would like nothing better than to push you out of it, especially if they observe that you have a weak hold on it or are doing nothing to strengthen your grip.' Once you have achieved your success, there is no time to rest on your laurels.

The market can be brutal to organizations that fail to evolve. Successful organizations today often become the pariahs and failures of tomorrow and in today's internet driven retail environment, the bastions of the high street can disappear with relative ease. Household names like Blockbuster, Enron, Arthur Andersen, Lehman Brothers and Borders are just a few examples of previously successful businesses going to the wall. The pundits that pick through the rubble of the retail and corporate failures often draw similar conclusions: the board refused to face up to the inevitable changes in the market; the organization was too slow to respond; the wrong decisions were made; the company over traded, mistimed or failed to predict demand; technology blindsided the organization; the hubris of the CEO led to disaster and the complacency of the company made the one-time market leader vulnerable to external competitive threats.

The same applies to individuals; how often do you see colleagues' stars rising one minute only to fall the next? Even at the more general level, how many times do we hear of employees who have given years of dedication to their company, kept their noses clean and built a solid reputation only to be discarded at the drop of a hat? Although much more personal, those who have become successful often exhibit similar traits as successful organizations. They believe they are better than they actually are; they are blindsided by those of equal or better capability; they assume they have the support of those around them and in particular those above them; they assume they have a future; and they too readily rest upon their laurels. From the foregoing it should be clear that holding onto your success, especially in the corporate world, can be precarious. And for those at or near the top of an organization, it can feel almost medieval, requiring constant vigilance to guard against the usurpers, pretenders and those who would like to take your place clipping at your heels.

So as much as Bristol's book is about achieving success, it is also about holding onto it.

DEFINING IDEA...

'Every person who wins in any undertaking must be willing to cut all sources of retreat. Only by doing so can one be sure of maintaining that state of mind known as a burning desire to win – essential to success.'
NAPOLEON HILL, MOTIVATIONAL AUTHOR

HERE'S AN IDEA FOR YOU...

Consider what you need or perhaps should do to hold on to the success you have already achieved. Are you confident that your skills, capabilities and networks are up to date and being refreshed periodically? Take some deliberate actions to ensure that your success is as secure as it can be.

4 MOULDED BY OTHERS

'We are moulded also by the thoughts of others; by what we hear in our social life, what we read in newspapers, magazines, and on the radio; even by chance remarks from the conversation of bystanders – and these bombard us constantly.' To be successful, we need to be selective when it comes to who we pay attention to.

As we grow up we are moulded into who we become by, amongst others, our parents, our childhood experiences, and our teachers. They exert a powerful influence over us as we develop and, irrespective of whether they are positive or negative, they set our future path. Although we might like to think that once we are adults external influences such as those experienced during childhood disappear, it is surprising to realize that we continue to be moulded by all sorts of things, albeit usually more subtly. Bristol also understood that whilst some of the things that influenced us were positive, others were negative and these had the ability to weaken our self-confidence. As children we could do little about them, but as adults we can choose whether or not to act on those that seek to influence and control us.

There are many occasions where a throwaway comment from someone you respect and even someone who you don't is able to kill off an idea before it has even got off the ground. Those around us throw cold water on our ideas for a whole number of reasons including jealousy, ignorance or just plain thoughtlessness. What we have to do is think carefully about the value of their comments and act accordingly. Rather than be influenced by what they say, use it as a spur to drive you on or consider the intentions behind what was said.

The same thing applies to what we read and what we hear. Stories printed in the press and broadcast on the news can also influence our thinking more heavily than we are aware. Celebrities can change our opinions on such things as fashion, politics and world issues. Although typically not experts in any of these things, their celebrity status has enormous sway over a large percentage of the population because of something called the halo effect. This involves accrediting the celebrity with skills they haven't got by dint of them being a celebrity; we assume them to be good at everything, when of course the reality is far from the truth. The best way to counter such influences on your life is to be well read, to learn to take other views into account, including those that might be counter to your own, and to be open minded. In this way you can weigh up what you hear, what you are told and what you read and act accordingly.

DEFINING IDEA...

'My father had a profound influence on me. He was a lunatic.'

SPIKE MILLIGAN, COMEDIAN

HERE'S AN IDEA FOR YOU...

Consider who influences you; this might include your spouse, your boss, or a celebrity. As you list them assess how much of an influence each has on your life and why, and think about whether the level of influence you allow them to have is justified.

5 SLEEP ON IT

After an evening of strenuous mental deliberation you often wake the next morning to find 'a mental picture of your problem – completely solved with all the directions for appropriate action'. Like that well-known fairy tale, a mysterious group of elves seem to have been in your workshop and finished your work overnight.

In *The Magic of Believing* Bristol presents the subconscious and its mysterious activities in much the same way. At first it seems rather ridiculous, but the more we consider it the more it accounts for the strange workings of our minds. How often are we advised to 'sleep on it' when faced with an important and difficult decision? Perhaps we don't stop to consider what's meant by this strange nugget of folk wisdom, or maybe we take it to mean 'stop worrying and think about it tomorrow'. Perhaps this is all it means. But how often have you gone to bed dejected, unable to solve a problem or come to a decision, only to awake the following morning and find the answer already in your mind?

Bristol's idea is that the conscious and subconscious minds work in different ways. We might take up a problem with our everyday, conscious mind and scrutinize it intently, employing logic and judgement, turning it this way and that, considering it from all angles, only to find ourselves even more confused than before. Perhaps, suggests Bristol, we're using the wrong tools for the job. By contrast the subconscious works beyond our understanding and control. The best we can do is feed it data, like a computer, and facilitate its workings, which largely means leaving it to it.

A 2006 study came to a strikingly similar conclusion. Studying the buying decisions and satisfaction rates of shoppers it found that the conscious mind was ideal for considering everyday items like washing powders and breakfast cereals. But bigger purchases – like buying a new car or house – require more complex thinking about the pros, cons, requirements and conditions. The most satisfied shoppers for these goods were those who had allowed the subconscious mind time to churn through the options and come up with an answer in its own time.

Of course we shouldn't give up thinking logically altogether and go with the flow of this mysterious subconscious. It's about balance. The conscious mind serves us perfectly well most of the time, but we need to know when to let go of our incessant worrying about more complex problems. After all, we know how to breathe without thinking about it. All Bristol is asking of us is that we realize the inherent power at our disposal – the power of the subconscious – and that we learn to utilize it effectively when situations demand.

DEFINING IDEA...

'To make a practical use of this instinct in every part of life constitutes true wisdom, and we must form the habit of preferring in all cases its guidance, which is given as it is used.'
RALPH WALDO EMERSON

HERE'S AN IDEA FOR YOU...

Some of us find ourselves still awake in the early hours trying desperately to find answers to daytime worries. Instead, try putting these worries to rest before bed by writing out all the considerations that are whizzing round your head. Now, with a decluttered mind allow yourself to drift off. On waking write up the thoughts that are foremost in your mind. In all likelihood a fresh perspective and clarity will have emerged from your subconscious during the night.

6 THE LIFELINE

Knowing that we will eventually die should spur us on to make the most of what time we have.

When Thomas Hobbes wrote *Leviathan* in 1651, he described the life of man as, 'solitary, poor, nasty, brutish, and short'. Others too took a somewhat dim view of life, including Pope Innocent III, who penned the cheery tome *On the Misery of the Human Condition* during the 1190s. Such people were not high on Bristol's list of inspirational role models and he recommended that you shouldn't spend too much time around those with negative outlooks. The reason he believed this to be the case was that the power of suggestion can work both ways and can be negative as well as positive. In studying Hitler, Mussolini and Stalin, who were able to persuade their countries to embark on a path of near annihilation during World War II, he could see how the repeated suggestion, imagery and slogans used by the dictators were capable of establishing powerful, if destructive, collective belief systems.

Although Bristol's perspective is helpful, perhaps there is something to take away from those who look on life as a form of purgatory and that's a resolution to make the most out of it. After all, one of the very few certainties in life is death. The fact that we die is actually a good thing in so far as it spurs us on to great things. Knowing that you have a finite time on Earth creates a sense of urgency to get things done. It could be argued that without this, the human race may not have achieved all it has done to date. Knowing that we will eventually die does not stop people, especially the rich, from wanting to live forever of course, but as Jonathan Swift points out in *Gulliver's Travels* it's not quite as fun as it sounds. In Luggnagg, Gulliver meets the Struldbrugs, a race of people who live forever. They do not have eternal youth, though, and so grow weaker and unhappier as they get older. Instead, we should embrace life and, in recognizing our time as relatively short, aim to spend it wisely in the realization of our dreams.

DEFINING IDEA...

'When one door closes, another opens; but we often look so long and so regretfully upon the closed door that we do not see the one that has opened for us.'

ALEXANDER GRAHAM BELL, INVENTOR

HERE'S AN IDEA FOR YOU...

Take a piece of paper and draw a horizontal line from one end to the other. This represents your life from birth to death. Then place a mark on the line which represents where you are now (i.e. your age). Consider how much time you might have left and think about what you want to achieve before you reach the end. From this, list all those things you would like to do, but never seem to have the time for. You may find this helps you find it.

7 THE POWER OF TALISMANS

Bristol recognizes the strong power that charms and trinkets – from a rabbit's foot to old horseshoes – can exert on thousands of people's lives. 'By themselves they are inanimate harmless objects ... but when people breathe life into them by their thinking they do have power ... The power comes only with the believing – which alone makes them effective.'

In June 1098 the First Crusade had reached a turning point. Having fought long and hard for eight months to gain entry into Antioch, a major stronghold and staging post on the way to Jerusalem, the Franks had rapidly gone from the besiegers to the besieged. No sooner had they gained access to the citadel than a massive Turkish army under Kerbogha arrived and placed them under constant attack for the next four weeks. Conditions deteriorated significantly and the losses combined with a lack of food and water began to take their toll on morale. Things looked very bad and annihilation seemed inevitable. Then a peasant named Peter Bartholomew shared a vision with the leaders of the Franks about the location of the Holy Lance (the one which had pierced Christ whilst on the cross). After digging into the night, the lance was found inside the walls of Antioch. With morale restored and a renewed sense of belief and purpose, the Franks took the fight to Kerbogha and against all odds managed to rout the Turks. Even though it is highly unlikely that Peter Bartholomew found the Holy Lance, the belief that it was a sacred artefact was sufficient to turn a seemingly inevitable disaster into a huge success.

Bristol cites Alexander the Great and Napoleon as prime examples of how a talisman can generate the basis of a self-fulfilling prophesy. By cutting the Gordian Knot, Alexander believed he would become the ruler of Asia as the prophesy predicted. As a child, Napoleon was given a star sapphire which came with the prediction that the holder would become Emperor of France; it seems likely he developed the sense of purpose and self-belief that allowed him to do just that. The question of course, is whether either would have been as successful without their respective talismans; this is something we will never know.

It is surprising how many of us use talismans, especially sportsmen and women. Although it is easy to dismiss such objects as having no intrinsic power, we should remember what Bristol said — it's not the object itself but rather the belief that comes with it that matters.

DEFINING IDEA...

'Courage and perseverance have a magical talisman, before which difficulties disappear and obstacles vanish into air.'

JOHN QUINCY ADAMS, 6TH US PRESIDENT

HERE'S AN IDEA FOR YOU...

You may not have an object that could be classed as a talisman, but consider what other objects you use. It may be a particular suit, lucky coin or something similar. Very often we attach beliefs to such objects without really knowing it. If you do have objects think about what this says about you and your beliefs.

8 TRUMPING INTIMIDATION

Intimidating people are not as overpowering as you think.

When was the last time you felt intimidated by someone? Most likely it was at work and more than likely it was your boss or someone in authority, such as the chief executive officer, for example. We feel overpowered or perhaps emasculated by such people because they are in positions of power. Even when they don't abuse their position, we can still feel uneasy in their company. We project certain images and perceptions onto them, for example, that they are 'better' than we are, more powerful and so on. How we feel is of course part of the human condition and as such perfectly natural. We are conditioned to react to authority from an early age when we depend on authority figures such as our parents and teachers. The need to break away from authority figures as we grow up, and especially when we are teenagers, is one of the reasons why so many of us go through a rebellious stage; we need to establish ourselves in the world and leave the shadow of our parents. This is only a passing phase, as when we enter into the world of work, we resort to the hard wiring of deferring to those in authority and those who have more power than we do (perceived or otherwise). There is nothing unique in how we behave, such behaviour is also played out in the animal kingdom: just think about troops of monkeys or prides of lions where one male, the alpha male, dominates all others.

Bristol has some sage advice for us when dealing with intimidation. In two examples he demonstrates the power behind *The Magic of Believing*. In the first, a salesman in the investment bank where he worked was so in awe of a multimillionaire client that he felt unable to sell to him. Bristol asked if the salesman would feel intimidated if he saw the person concerned in his swimming trunks, to which the salesman of course said he wouldn't. The next time the salesman saw his client he used the mental image of him in his trunks and not only was he not intimidated, but he also sold him some securities. In the second example, a lawyer felt frightened when up against a more experienced and well known lawyer in court. In this instance, rather than using mental imagery as the salesman had done, he used an affirmation and told himself that he was not only as good as this lawyer, but better. By repeating this a few times, he believed it and no longer felt intimidated. Bristol sums up by saying, 'Just bear in mind that these executives are mere human beings with the same fears, the same frailties, the same faults that are common to millions …'.

DEFINING IDEA …

'Leadership is based on inspiration, not domination; on cooperation, not intimidation.'

WILLIAM ARTHUR WARD, AMERICAN AUTHOR AND PASTOR

HERE'S AN IDEA FOR YOU …

The next time you feel intimidated by someone, paint a mental picture that is amusing. For example give them bright green hair, warts, clown's shoes and large rimmed glasses. Make the image as vivid and colourful as you can and very soon any intimidation you may feel will drop away.

9 YOUR BODY SPEAKS ITS MIND

Our minds and bodies are intimately linked. Bristol realized that 'What you exhibit outwardly, you are inwardly. You are the product of your own thought. What you believe yourself to be, you are.'

The fact that Bristol understood that the mind controls every facet of our daily lives, from picking up a newspaper to walking down the street, probably comes as no surprise to anyone who has read *The Magic of Believing*. Perhaps what does surprise is his assertion that rather than being a slave to our minds in the automaton sense, we can actually have more control over them and, as a consequence, over our own destinies. Bristol helped to begin to shift our thinking away from the idea that we are dealt a set of cards in life towards a belief in which we are masters of our own destinies. And although his book was written long before neurolinguistic programming (NLP) came along, it was a major step forward in helping us understand the links between our brain and our physiology. Such links are now well known, as is our ability to pick up the subtleties of body language. Whether it is during romantic encounters or during board meetings, body language always comes into play.

'A slovenly carriage,' notes Bristol, 'is an indication of slovenly thinking, whereas an alert, upright carriage is the outward sign of inward strength and confidence.' Similarly, we can usually tell if someone likes or dislikes us, whether they are lying or telling the truth and whether they are confident or shy. One modern theory suggests that our bodies provide a complete window on our minds. The idea behind this is that our bodies develop in direct response to our psychological development as we grow up and by the time we are seven things are pretty much set for adulthood. The five archetypes of wizard, poet, superhero, good parent and warrior (plus combinations of each) view the world in a particular way and their bodies reflect their psychological make-up. For example, the warrior, as the name suggests is athletic, competitive and driven; winning matters to them. The superhero archetype has a powerful ego and self-belief which manifests itself as a need to save the world, a business or a damsel in distress. Their body reflects their huge ego by way of an oversized upper body with tiny legs (just like Mr Incredible from the cartoon movie *The Incredibles*). It is clear that how you think affects your body in many different ways, so it is worth paying attention to.

DEFINING IDEA...

'The human body is the best picture of the human soul.'

LUDWIG WITTGENSTEIN, PHILOSOPHER

HERE'S AN IDEA FOR YOU...

Spend some time studying body language – there are plenty of good books on the subject. Consider how you can use your own body language to further your goals and use your newly gained knowledge to pay closer attention to those people you need to influence.

10 APPEAL BY DRAMA

Bristol says: 'The very way you walk, the way you carry yourself, your talk, your manner of dress, all reflect your way of thinking... What you exhibit outwardly, you are inwardly.'

Shakespeare's Richard III is considered one of the greatest villains in fiction. The playwright depicts him as a bitter rogue who takes it upon himself to 'prove a villain' in answer to the unfair lot he feels life has dealt him. His mind has become victim to his physical deformity; in the now time-honoured tradition of villainy, Richard's deformed appearance reflects his inner wretchedness and propensity for vengeful scheming. Had Richard read *The Magic of Believing* it may well have been a different story. Bristol highlights the connection between thought and manner. Instead of being victim to either our habitual thoughts or actions we can take control of both and play the person we want to be. In the playing we not only alter how we think about ourselves but learn the skill of convincing others too.

Proof of the connection between belief and comportment is all around us. Shy people often avoid making eye contact and may fold their arms as if to shield themselves from the outside world. Confident people, on the other hand, have a relaxed and open body language and hold their heads high. So we inadvertently give off signals about what we think about ourselves. Similarly, we pick up on signals given off by others and reach snap judgements about them. This in turn affects how we act towards them, reinforcing the validity of our roles in the relationship.

So the circle continues, resulting in the establishment of characters that appear rigid and unchangeable.

The connection between mind and body is so strong that the relationship can work in reverse. If we put on an act for long enough we can create affirmative beliefs, and become what we always wanted to be. If we carry ourselves confidently we are likely to form the belief that we are naturally confident. We dress to impress for interviews and make an extra effort to carry ourselves in a confident, professional manner. To start with we may feel we are lying about ourselves, as our body language masks the inner turmoil of our anxieties. But after a while we find ourselves taking on this confident persona more readily and become our character just as an actor becomes the part he plays. Our anxieties cease, convinced wholeheartedly by the confidence our body expresses. This confidence in turn will affect others because, as Bristol says, an 'appeal by drama is the first step in arousing the emotions of people.' Once their emotions are engaged, their belief will follow close behind.

DEFINING IDEA...

'Assume a virtue if you have it not.'

SHAKESPEARE

HERE'S AN IDEA FOR YOU...

Even the most important and successful executives are no more or less human than you. They too have dreams and fears, and are just as susceptible to the powerful beliefs of others. If you believe yourself to be inferior then this is how you will come across. Instead, act confidently in their presence and inspire reciprocal respect. With their respect will come your own self-belief.

11 CONNECTING THE DOTS

Janus looked forward as well as back. So should we.

In ancient Roman religion and mythology, Janus is the god of beginnings and transitions, capable of looking forward as well as back. There was a Janus-like quality to Bristol's life insofar as he not only looked forward by setting his mind to becoming wealthy, but he also looked back and joined up the dots to understand his journey. This helped him to see that once he had set his mind to it, everything that had happened to him from that point on had led him to becoming wealthy. This notion of joining up the dots is a central takeaway from *The Magic of Believing* because it reinforces the importance of having faith in your beliefs.

Steve Jobs was an inspiration to millions of people around the world and as the founder of Apple, the iconic brand and multibillion dollar success story, he changed the way we view computers from being something somewhat functional to something artistic and sexy. Jobs died in October 2011 of a rare form of pancreatic cancer and although very ill, he continued to drive the Apple brand right to the end. In 2005 he gave a speech at the Stanford graduation ceremony which was nothing short of inspirational. He told three stories, of which one chimes with Bristol's *The Magic of Believing*. This related to how he came to set up Apple and why joining the dots was so important.

Jobs was given up for adoption by his unmarried mother in 1955. When offering up her unborn child she insisted that the parents were graduates and that they would ensure her child went to university. When Jobs was born the selected parents, who were both graduates, chose not to have him because they wanted a daughter. As a result he was offered up to another couple who were both non-graduates, much to the chagrin of his mother. In due course he went to Stanford University, but the combination of the costs which his adopted parents had to pay and a lack of interest in his course resulted in him dropping out. As a dropout however, he still hung around campus and took courses that interested him, one of which was calligraphy, which he found fascinating. Ten years later, when he was setting up Apple and designing the first Apple Mac, the calligraphy course came into its own when he put form and design at heart of Apple. And from this, Apple grew to be the iconic organization that millions now love. Jobs firmly believed that his success relied on his belief that at some point all the dots would join up and that gave him the confidence to pursue his heart, rather than just collect a pay cheque.

DEFINING IDEA...

'You can't connect the dots looking forward; you can only connect them looking backwards. So you have to trust that the dots will somehow connect in your future. You have to trust in something – your gut, destiny, life, karma, whatever. This approach has never let me down, and it has made all the difference in my life.'

STEVE JOBS – FOUNDER OF APPLE

HERE'S AN IDEA FOR YOU...

Spend some time looking back on your career and see if you can connect the dots to see how your various roles and job moves have led to where you are today. Then consider if this is where you wanted to be. If not, what can you learn from your past to help you plot a better route in the future.

12 IF YOU BELIEVE IT, WRITE IT DOWN

It is always better to write down your goals.

Bristol was very clear on what you had to do if you were to get what you wanted out of life. There was no point in having some vague notion of what you wanted, like being successful or being rich for example. Instead, he believed that you had to have a very clear mental picture. He also recommended that you ask yourself a series of questions to ensure it was fully defined, such as where am I headed? What is my goal? Have I visualized just what I really want? He believed that the answers to these questions contained the factors which framed the rest of your life. Bristol was always amazed and somewhat disappointed to find that very few people were able to answer the questions above when asked. In his mind, such people 'are like a cork on the water floating aimlessly, drawn this way and that by various currents, and either being washed up on the shore, or becoming waterlogged and eventually sinking.' The only way to be successful is to know exactly what you want out of life, to know where you are headed and to have the goal fixed and always in view.

So it's clear that you need to set yourself well defined goals and keep them at the front of your mind. To be truly effective, it's always best to write them down. Much has been written about the 1953 Yale University goals study in which students were tracked following graduation. Those who had committed their goals to paper were significantly more successful and wealthier than those who hadn't. In fact, it seems that the study never really happened, even though it entered into the subconscious of the management thinkers of the time. One study by the Dominican University in California, however, did prove that writing goals down made a difference. How so? The benefit lies in the physiology of the brain. The act of writing stimulates a group of cells which lie at the base of the brain, called the reticular activating system or RAS. The RAS acts as a filter which ensures that the brain focuses on the things it needs to and ignores the rest. Whatever you are focusing on is given more importance and once the brain has received its instructions it will work on their execution. Consider the act of writing your goals down as *The Magic of Believing* on steroids. And one final tip, always capture your goals in the past tense as though they have already happened.

DEFINING IDEA...

'Goals in writing are dreams with deadlines.'

BRIAN TRACY, MOTIVATIONAL SPEAKER

HERE'S AN IDEA FOR YOU...

Commit to putting your goals in writing. When doing so, why not use the SMART (Specific, Measurable, Achievable, Realistic and Time based) approach to documenting them to ensure they are sufficiently 'real'. Once you have written them down, revisit them periodically to remind yourself of what they are and to track progress.

13 MENTAL MODELS

How we relate to the world around us is largely defined by our internal mental model.

The Magic of Believing is all about how we define success internally and use our subconscious mind to help us to achieve what we want in life. It is such a simple and indeed compelling idea that everyone ought to be able to do it, and yet the fact that comparatively few actually do suggests that it is not necessarily that easy to achieve. Indeed, throughout the book Bristol highlights the often sceptical responses he got from those who believed he was selling something that wasn't attainable. Unwrapping this dichotomy leads to the conclusion that if we really do want to be successful then we have to have a mental model that is success oriented. For some, this comes naturally, but for others it requires that we change our existing mental models to ones which are more positive.

There is a German word that sums up what this is all about – Weltanschauung. The word is a combination of Welt (the world) and Anschauung (view) and is a central pillar of German philosophy. It refers to the framework of ideas and beliefs through which we interpret and interact with the world around us. Our own world view forms as we grow up and is defined by the combination of such things as the culture in which we live, our family environment, school, work and so on. It is also defined by our experiences and eventually becomes a powerful tool through which we 'see' the world around us; it forms the core of our belief system. It also acts as a lens through which we filter information and the events we experience, rejecting those things which are not part of our world view and accepting those which are.

The beliefs we hold are in many respects our truths – the things we hold to be true for us and no other. To illustrate just how powerful they can be, we only need to look at what happened to Cortez when he landed in the New World. When he arrived off the coast of Mexico in 1519 he encountered some fisherman busying themselves about their daily lives. What surprised Cortez was their response – they ignored the huge Spanish Galleons which were a few hundred metres from the shore and carried on fishing. They apparently did not 'see' them because such vessels were not part of their belief system. In other words they didn't believe that such things existed; why should they? This demonstrates that we do not so much believe what we see, but see what we believe and that is what *The Magic of Believing* is all about.

DEFINING IDEA...

'Whether you think that you can, or that you can't, you are usually right.'

HENRY FORD, AMERICAN INDUSTRIALIST

HERE'S AN IDEA FOR YOU...

What are your core beliefs and universal truths? Write them down and use them to build a picture of your world view. When you have done this, consider whether it is aligned to your life and career goals and where necessary consider changing it.

14 SEEK AND YOU SHALL FIND

Once you have set your mind on something it's funny how everything gravitates towards it.

There is a fascinating video clip that in some respects demonstrates the power of belief, but not necessarily in the way you would expect. The video involves a number of people on a basketball court throwing a ball between them. Observers watching the video are asked to count the number of times the ball is thrown between the players. Midway through the experiment a man in a gorilla suit saunters across the court, momentarily stops, beats his chest, and then continues until he reaches the other side and disappears from sight. When the observers are asked how many times the ball has been thrown they usually get the answer correct. However, when they are asked if they saw the gorilla over 50 per cent said they hadn't seen anything but the ball being thrown. When the gorilla is pointed out to them, they cannot believe they missed it. Cognitive psychologists call this selective attention and it explains why when focused on a task or goal we usually ignore everything that is irrelevant to it even when it is as significant as a gorilla walking across a basketball court. There are many other experiments that illustrate the same concept and taken together they illustrate just how powerful the mind is at focusing on something so completely that everything else is excluded.

This also works in a positive way, and this is where *The Magic of Believing* comes into play. When you set your mind on something and have a strong desire to make it happen, it acts like a magnet. For example, an experienced journalist researching a particular topic is typically able to bring to mind relevant newspaper articles and snippets from books and journals without any prompting. In fact everyone will have experienced this at some time. Without conscious planning you can find yourself opening a book at random and being drawn straight to a word or phrase that chimes perfectly with your particular interest, as if Fate herself had drawn you to that exact page. Similarly when reading the newspaper we seem to have inadvertently trained our minds to pick out relevant stories, like and eagle scanning its environment for prey. Choice nuggets seem to spring out of the page at us. Like the eagle we can come to trust the power of our subconscious in our everyday lives.

Bristol was certain that thousands of successful men and women had reached great heights and accomplished marvellous results thanks to the applied power of the subconscious. Thanks to *The Magic of Believing*, we can now harness its power for ourselves.

DEFINING IDEA...
'I was like a boy playing on the sea-shore, and diverting myself now and then, finding a smoother pebble or a prettier shell than ordinary, whilst the great ocean of truth lay all undiscovered before me.'
SIR ISAAC NEWTON

HERE'S AN IDEA FOR YOU...
The next time you have a difficult task to complete, or a particular goal to achieve, have faith that your subconscious mind will help you achieve it. If you give it time to weave its magic, you will be surprised when the answer suddenly pops into your mind, often when you least expect it

15 THE INNER GAME

To unlock your true potential you have to turn down the volume of your inner voice.

The underlying tenet of *The Magic of Believing* is that the power to realize your full potential lies within your mind. Compelling as this is, as we will see in Idea 32, too many of us throw up unnecessary barriers and obstacles that prevent us from getting what we truly want in life. We also spend far too much time ruminating over setbacks, which is equally debilitating. In quoting the French philosopher Theodore Simon Jouffroy, 'The subconscious mind will not take the trouble to work for those who don't believe in it', Bristol makes it clear that to be successful we have to believe in the power of our minds; if we don't, then we won't be as successful as we want to be. One way to address this tendency for us to sabotage our own success is to master what is known as the inner game.

The inner game has been popularized by Timothy Gallwey, who developed the idea as a sports coach. Very simply the inner game is about the internal conversations that occur within your head between what Gallwey terms Self 1 and Self 2. Self 1 is the stern, know-it-all who issues commands and judges the results. This is the inner conversation that says 'you haven't finished this yet' or 'I'm not sure if this is a good idea'. Self 1 is generally untrusting of Self 2. Self 2 is the human being itself which is packed with natural potential as well as the skills and capabilities to achieve most things. Our ability to realize our potential depends heavily on our ability to limit the controlling Self 1 and allowing Self 2 to carry out the tasks in hand in a calm and natural manner. Gallwey noticed this during coaching sessions with tennis players and later with golfers. By focusing the judgemental Self 1 on just one component of the ball, such as its speed for example, he found that a player's Self 2 would take over and make a perfect hit. Thus turning down the volume of Self 1 was key to success in improving the game. This is similar to the state of flow that we sometimes reach when we are so focused on a task that time flies and we seem to tackle it effortlessly. The inner game is an excellent way to manage your internal dialogue and well worth the effort wherever you apply it; in the office or on the golf course.

DEFINING IDEA...

'When we plant a rose seed in the earth, we notice that it is small, but we do not criticize it as rootless and stemless.'

TIMOTHY GALLWEY, SPORTS COACH AND AUTHOR

HERE'S AN IDEA FOR YOU...

I am sure you have your inner voice; always niggling away at you when you do things. Try to apply Gallwey's ideas to the things you do; it doesn't matter whether it is work, relationship or sport related. See if you can distract your untrusting Self 1 so that Self 2 can get on with the task in hand.

16 THE POWER OF PHYSIOLOGY

Your body can have an amazing effect on your mind and your mind can have amazing effects on your body.

Although Bristol's *The Magic of Believing* is focused on the power of the subconscious mind he also recognizes the significance of physiology on your mental state. In many respects you cannot separate the two. For example, shut your eyes and slump in a chair as though you are tired and lack energy. Do it for long enough and you will find that your mind begins to shut down and reinforces the physical effect; after a while you won't feel like getting out of your chair. Bristol uses the example of soldiers standing to attention, sticking out their chest and breathing deeply – not only do they look confident, they feel it too. The mind jumps to attention along with the body.

There is a strong association between our psychological state and our physical state; indeed, physiology can dramatically improve our ability to realize our goals. According to the latest research, our ability to master and remember new things is improved by the biological changes in the brain brought about by physical activity. Physical exercise can result in better and healthier brains, which in turn means we are better equipped to learn, overcome obstacles and achieve what we want in life. It is also well known that when we are anxious our frontal lobes shut down, limiting our ability to reason and address complex issues. The opposite is true when we are happy. Taking this one step further involves creating what is known as an anchor. An anchor is a mental image, word or other cue which we associate with a high performing state. Your anchor can be anything you like; an image from your past, a phrase that you can really identify with or just a particular stance you may hold. Associating this image with a 10 (your highest performance state) means that every time you want to be at a high performing state all you need to do is recall the image, replay the phrase or get into that position. Then you will be able to play from a 10 ... instantly.

DEFINING IDEA...

'Peak Performance is the fulfilment of potential. It can only be achieved by reaching maximum fitness of body and mind, of attitude and expectation. A Peak Performer is fit for any challenge, is mentally equipped to meet the challenge, approaches the challenge knowing that it can be met and certain that it will be completed.'

JIM STEELE, COLIN HILES AND MARTIN COBURN, MOTIVATIONAL AUTHORS

HERE'S AN IDEA FOR YOU...

If you want to feel more confident in dealing with your work colleagues, clients or perhaps even your spouse, consider how your body affects how you feel and how others perceive you. If you look and sound confident, you will be more believable and more likely to get your way. So the next time you are in a situation where you need to be more assertive and confident, stand upright, push your chest out and keep an open body stance.

17 THINK YOUR WORLD INTO BEING

'Your very life is your thinking and the result of your thinking processes. Your flesh, bones and muscle can be reduced to 70% water and a few chemicals of small value, but it is your mind that makes you what you are.' Bristol bases all of his conclusions and advice in *The Magic of Believing* on this simple, universally acknowledged premise.

Yet it's easy to believe that what we think doesn't really matter, that the world will continue as ever regardless of what we think and however much we'd like it to change. We feel powerless to make the changes we long for and at the end of another fruitless endeavour we comfort ourselves with the thought that there was nothing we could have done about it anyway.

But look around you: all the millions of objects around us originated from a thought. That chair or book or bus is really an idea made manifest in the material world. Some are quite simple, a table or a tray; others, like a Boeing 747, are complex and comprise lots of little ideas all working in harness. The same is true of the mightiest empires of the past, the most advanced cultures and the greatest human achievements. All began as ideas, as initial sparks of inspiration. Without ideas there would be no progress.

It's all too easy to think this doesn't apply to us. The fact is that all actions, from simple bodily movements to complex and moral actions, come about as the result of a preceding thought. Thought impulses typically feel like one-offs. They seem to arise from nowhere and disappear just as quickly. But really our impulses follow the same well-trodden paths day in, day out. The ways we think define the possibilities we see in our lives. Science concurs: the synapse connections that fire between the neurons in our brains develop established routes and then proceed to frequent those routes again and again. No wonder it's so hard to break out when our very thinking becomes constrained like this.

So our thoughts are really very powerful but, unaware of this, we let them work in ways that aren't always in our favour. Bristol wants us to realize that with effort we can harness this power and direct it towards our goals. Then our deepest desires would be within reach. This all sounds suspiciously simple and of course there's more to it than just wanting, but this is the vital first step. Once you realize that the thoughts that predominate in your life 'determine your character, your career, indeed your everyday life', then the power of what you think will open to you. By training yourself in helpful thinking you place your mind in a state to notice opportunity and work towards it in a positive way.

DEFINING IDEA...

'We are what we think. All that we are arises with our thoughts. With our thoughts we make the world.'

THE DHAMMAPADA

HERE'S AN IDEA FOR YOU...

Take a long, hard look at your everyday assumptions, about yourself and your future. How have you been thinking? If you assume your goals are miles away, then you will have been acting as if they are unachievable. Make a list of new goals and challenge yourself to achieve them within the year. Take baby-steps like this, forming habits around positive beliefs and the recognition of the positives in your life.

18 WHAT WOULD EDISON SAY?

Even the most successful people draw on the inspirations of others; so should we.

Long before Bristol developed the ideas behind *The Magic of Believing* he had the opportunity to spend time with many of the great and the good of his time and was often invited into their private offices. What he noticed was that most, if not all of them had motivational statements, pictures and occasionally statues and shrines in prominent places. For example Frank Winfield Woolworth the famous retailer was believed to have had a replica of Napoleon's library in his office. Edison often drew on the following statement he had written on a piece of paper which was found in his desk after his death: 'when down in the mouth, remember Jonah, he came out alright.' Bristol believed that the only reason they had such things was to serve as a constant reminder that they too could succeed as others had before them. Such sentiments are reflected in Newton's famous statement 'If I have seen further it is by standing on the shoulders of giants'. Newton acknowledged that he was only able to succeed because of the scientific endeavours and advances of those who went before him.

Organizations as well as individuals have come to understand the value of role models, motivational posters, slogans and inspirational speakers. They can have a powerful influence on their staff and productivity. For example, Olympic gold medallists are in high demand because of the stories they can tell; of the personal sacrifice, hard work, setbacks and ultimately success. The fact that someone from humble beginnings is able to win a gold medal demonstrates that anyone can succeed so long as they have the necessary self-belief and commitment. Many an athlete has been inspired to go for gold from watching the Olympics themselves and from the stories of Olympic success. And because athletes, film stars and other famous people hold such sway over the general population they are used to advertise products, support charity campaigns and even influence politicians.

One of the most powerful examples was the Lord Kitchener 'Your country needs you' poster that first appeared on the front cover of *London Opinion* magazine on September 5th 1914. September became the month which saw the highest number of volunteers signing up to join the army. Kitchener, who was appointed Secretary for the State for War on the outbreak of hostilities, was possibly the most recognized person in Britain following the posters and postcards that were produced as part of the recruitment campaign. Whether it was Kitchener himself that influenced so many to go off to war or the fact that wherever you stood he was pointing directly at you is not known, but it was incredibly effective.

DEFINING IDEA...

'I am a poor student sitting at the feet of giants, yearning for their wisdom and begging for lessons that might one day make me a complete artist, so that if all goes well, I may one day sit beside them.'

ROD TAYLOR, ACTOR

HERE'S AN IDEA FOR YOU...

Think about someone who could provide you with a powerful role model. It might be a sports personality, a business giant or someone else. Consider having a poster of them on the wall or one of their quotes on your desk so that you can see it or reference it when you need inspiration

19 BE UNFLAPPABLE

Bristol says: 'Far too many people are like little saplings that are swayed by every little breeze and ultimately grow in the direction of some strong wind of thought that blows against them'. The best thing is to be unflappable – in charge of your own beliefs and able to withstand the influence of others.

Metaphorical references to the natural world abound in Zen training literature. A solid rock, thoroughly grounded, is immovable no matter what the weather throws at it. The student is encouraged to develop an unshakeable presence, untroubled by daily difficulties. A Zen master is always able to maintain his composure. On meeting a disturbance he remains unaffected; like smoke blowing through brambles, he doesn't get snagged. This is the ability appealed to in *The Magic of Believing* – it's what will mark you out for success, as you unerringly pursue your goals, undaunted by fear and unshakable in your resolve.

This is a high ideal indeed, seemingly impossible to live up to but thoroughly worth striving for. Many of us feel as though we're wearing big woollen jumpers when we meet the brambles of doubt and uncertainty; we get snagged on this and that worry and the more we try to free ourselves the more entangled we become. Before we know it we're completely unable to move. This can happen despite all our good intentions and our belief in ourselves. So the power of your belief – that you will achieve your goals – has to be such that you can't fail. In fact this is impossible; you will fail sometimes and this knowledge should be built into your survival strategy. So rather than being immune to failing you have to be insensitive to the despair of failure. Your can-do attitude must shield you from despondency. It's not that the Zen master never meets difficulty, it's that he knows how to act when he does.

Even if you master your own inner critic there are always very real, very harsh critics waiting for you in the outside world. These may be the normal naysayers in your life; you probably know who they are. Then again they may be your nearest and dearest, who no doubt think they have your best interests at heart and want to save you from potential disaster. They might have fair comments and if they do take them on board. It's no good being unresponsive to good advice. The point is, once you've made a decision about what you want, you have to stand by it. Criticism has no more power than the power you give it. According to Bristol's theory, your belief can only take root in the subconscious, and the subconscious can only get to work on guiding you to achieve it if you stick by it. In that case you must become unflappable, no matter what the world throws at you.

DEFINING IDEA...

'Nothing gives one person so great advantage over another, as to remain always cool and unruffled under all circumstances.'
THOMAS JEFFERSON

HERE'S AN IDEA FOR YOU...

Try some mindful meditation to calm the mind and improve its ability to process effectively in times of crisis. Assume an upright posture and focus your attention on your breath as it moves in and out of the nostrils. See if you can count ten breaths without losing your concentration. If you find yourself lost in thought, return to one and try again. Practising this once a day can help you stay on top of your chattering mind and keep your composure throughout the day.

20 HARD WORK IS NOT ENOUGH

Being successful is more than just hard work ... but what is it?

What makes people successful is something that intrigues us all and is one of the few things that can consistently sell millions of books and pack out conference halls. Just consider Steven Covey's *The 7 Habits of Highly Effective People* which has sold more than 25 million copies in 38 languages worldwide; it remains one of the bestselling non-fiction books of all time. When we read Covey's book we like to think that if we apply his seven principles we too will be effective.

It is a well-known fact that hard work alone is not enough to be successful. If you look at the most successful people in society, they are not always the smartest or indeed the hardest working; they have other attributes that seem to set them apart and make them successful. This is why we are so interested in them and why so many management gurus and authors take the time and effort to distil their findings into applicable lists of five, seven or ten things that make the successful, successful. A quick internet search on 'what makes people successful' offers over 85 million results – a useful measure of the demand for such answers.

One example from Alex Banayan, who spent a year interviewing the world's most successful people, suggested that there were five key attributes: the audacity to break the rules; an irrational level of commitment; a hunger to solve problems; a ferocious drive to do more; and a sharp focus on playing the people game. Other gurus have their own lists of attributes. The reason why we are so interested in such opinions and are willing to spend literally millions on books on the topic of success is that we all want the short-cuts that will get us there faster. If only it were that simple.

Bristol made himself familiar with the lives of the great men and women of history and over the course of his life he interviewed many outstanding people. He often wondered what it was that propelled them to the top of their game, be it politics, sport or business. Gradually he discovered by reading about religions, cults and the physical and mental sciences that there was a golden thread which ran through everything. And that golden thread was belief. It was this that allowed some people to climb the ladder of success. So perhaps in the end searching for the five, seven or ten pointers to success may be rather like seeking the pot of gold at the end of a rainbow; futile, as success ultimately lies within.

DEFINING IDEA…

'The difference between a successful person and others is not a lack of strength, not a lack of knowledge, but rather a lack of will.'

VINCE LOMBARDI, AMERICAN FOOTBALL COACH

HERE'S AN IDEA FOR YOU…

Consider that there are no short-cuts to success. So instead of seeking out the latest research that captures the behaviours that make people successful, define what success means for you in your own terms. You may well find that what makes others successful is different to what makes you successful and as a result you may find it easier to achieve.

21 THE FOUNDATIONS OF TRUST

Bristol exhorts us to lag the foundations of trust by developing a reputation for reliability. 'If you tell another person that you are going to do a certain thing, even though its fulfilment may cause you some inconvenience, do it no matter what the consequences or the cost in time or energy.'

Let's face it, nobody likes someone who fails to keep their word. Sure we may give them the benefit of the doubt once, but when they repeatedly let you down, they become branded as unreliable and are given a wide berth.

It is well known that it takes a long time and a lot of effort to build a solid reputation and very little to lose it. Bristol was fully aware of this and summed up the issue nicely when relaying a conversation he had with the personnel manager of a defence organization. The biggest fault the personnel manager found in people was that they could not be depended upon. He went on to say, 'Some fail to keep their word, others are always late for their engagements, still others are always changing their minds.' Bristol advises that keeping your word and fulfilling expectation is vital if you want to progress, 'You will be amply repaid, for you are building a reputation for reliability, which will be of great value as you proceed up the ladder.'

This is an important point as, even if you want to be successful and use the tools and techniques suggested by Bristol, you still need others to help you along the way. The best way to garner support from others is to build a strong personal brand firmly based upon reliability. With this, people will trust you and be willing to become your advocates.

21 THE FOUNDATIONS OF TRUST

At its simplest level trust is based upon the following three principles and if you can live up to these, then you will earn the respect and trust of those around you.

Achieving results – first and foremost, people trust those who are willing (because of their drive, discipline and commitment) and able (because of their knowledge, skills and courage) to deliver the results they promise. By contrast, we distrust those we consider misguided or incompetent.

Acting with integrity – integrity requires honesty in one's words and consistency in one's actions. People trust those who are direct in expressing their views and predictable in acting within a known set of principles. Inconsistency suggests that people are dishonest or self-serving. Those who conceal or distort the truth, or who constantly change their strategies and practices, are rarely trusted.

Demonstrating concern – fundamentally, trust requires that we understand and respect the interests of people at all levels and in all constituencies. More specifically, people trust those who consider their interests even in the face of potentially conflicting pressures.

DEFINING IDEA...

'It is easier to do one's duty to others than to one's self. If you do your duty to others, you are considered reliable. If you do your duty to yourself, you are considered selfish.'

THOMAS SZASZ, AMERICAN PSYCHOLOGIST

HERE'S AN IDEA FOR YOU...

What actions could you take to generate a reputation for reliability? A good way to start is to measure yourself against the three principles outlined above and if you are particularly brave, ask your colleagues to give you honest feedback. Why not develop an action plan once you have gathered your feedback?

22 THINK THE BEST OF OTHERS

'You wager, think and believe that the other fellow is a fine chap, and that's what he'll turn out to be,' says Bristol in a statement with clear moral ramifications. While the system of mental cause and effect can be used to achieve personal goals, the other side of the coin is the goodness it can spread to other people's lives and the increased benefits that return to us.

It will be clear by now that what we believe has the potential to produce positive effects in the world around us. We might be natural cynics and get caught in the trap of wondering what's in it for us; it's a dog-eat-dog world out there. But Bristol makes clear that once we consider the cause and effect, the give and take of our relationships with others, we see the folly of such cynical outlooks. Relationships are reciprocal; we get back what we give. If we only take one thing away from *The Magic of Believing* it should be the realization that we are in charge of what we believe. It's always worth being friendly to others because as Bristol says, 'what you get back is a reflection of what you project'.

Not only can we control the signals we transmit about ourselves and emphasize our good qualities – our friendliness, diligence and reliability (qualities that are likely to help us succeed in our work and social lives) – but we can also take control of the impressions we form of others.

We often take a dislike to someone based on something insignificant. They might have said something unfair about us; they might have looked at us in a funny way. Wherever an impression comes from it tends to stick in our minds as an unchangeable fact. We even take the unintended gestures of others and regard them as true representations of their personalities. We'd be mortified to discover that others did the same for us. We might think that it's 'not our problem'. But it is – what good can come of poor relationships, either at work or play? And how often have we been proved wrong in our judgements anyway? An 'enemy' compliments us and in a flash all our bad feeling evaporates. Clearly we have the power to turn things around and once we do we radiate a positivity that is infectious. Others become more receptive to our influence and more forgiving of our mistakes. On a basic level we recognize the humanity in each other and realize the mutual benefit of co-operation over conflict. 'Watch the bus driver respond, the elevator operator beam, and the clerk behind the counter hurry to oblige you when you send out friendly thoughts. It can be used in every encounter in life... Fortunate is he who is able to make a friend of an enemy'.

DEFINING IDEA...

'Treat others as you treat yourself'

MAHĀBHĀRATA, ANCIENT INDIAN TEXT

HERE'S AN IDEA FOR YOU...

Reconsider your impressions of the people in your life. Have you written some of them off unfairly? Even if you think some people deserve the cold shoulder, why not give them another chance? If you work to alter the way you habitually treat others and give them the benefit of the doubt you may well find they do the same for you. If they don't, at least you know you tried and you can get on with your life without worry.

23 KNOW YOUR LIMITATIONS

Success comes easily, so long as you build your capabilities and plan ahead.

In the Dirty Harry films Clint Eastwood played the maverick police inspector 'Dirty' Harry Callahan, an uncompromising San Francisco cop. In dispensing justice to criminals in and around the city, Callahan came out with some great one liners. Film fans will recognize, 'feeling lucky, punk?' and 'a good man knows his limitations'. Both provide an insight into the way Bristol wanted his book and ideas to be applied.

As those who came up against Dirty Harry often found out, relying on pure luck just doesn't cut it. Bristol was keen to remind the reader that his book was not an overnight open-sesame to riches and fame. His techniques were intended only as a key to unlock the door; the reader must have the courage and determination to walk through it. He counselled readers against rushing into undertakings which were far beyond their capabilities or their development. So, although *The Magic of Believing* is all about the power of suggestion and the subconscious mind, Bristol is at pains to point out that it is not just about random, lucky events. It actually takes deliberate well-planned steps in combination with training your subconscious to become acutely focused on your goals.

There is of course some degree of luck with most things, as we should recognize that you cannot plan for absolutely everything. As Bill Gates said when talking about the success of Microsoft, 'The timing wasn't entirely luck, but without great luck it wouldn't have happened.'

Bristol was equally clear that we should know our limitations. As he pointed out in his advice to the reader, 'If you would be the head of a great utility concern, you would naturally have to know the business, just as you would if you aspired to become the head of a huge transportation system.' In other words, you cannot realize your goals without doing your homework, building your capabilities, making deliberate career moves and planning ahead. As he said, 'You wouldn't go into the corner drugstore and ask just for drugs. You would be specific and name the drugs desired. And so it is with this science. You must have a plan of action – you've got to know what you want and be specific about it.' Success requires that we both understand where our knowledge and capability gaps lie and take actions to close them.

It is clear that Bristol was not selling snake oil or indeed a fast track to fame and fortune, unlike some gurus and all Ponzi schemes. Instead he was offering an approach through which you could channel your capabilities, desires, goals and objectives so that you could increase the likelihood of achieving your life and career goals.

DEFINING IDEA...

'The more I practise the luckier I get.'

GARY PLAYER, GOLFER

HERE'S AN IDEA FOR YOU...

How do you make your own luck? Consider how forward planning in terms of your career, skill and capability development and so on helps to develop an environment where luck is less random and more expected.

24 NO ONE IS AN ISLAND

To be successful usually requires a little help from our friends.

Culture is a fascinating subject, especially when looked at from an international perspective. Although national cultures can be viewed across a number of different dimensions one of the most useful is its degree of collectivism. National cultures which are considered to be more collective are dominated by the family unit and society is typically controlled by a small number of powerful families. Success in life is largely determined by your family ties and who you know rather than what you know. You cannot succeed without engaging the right people or gaining sponsorship and support from those with influence and power. In those societies that are considered more individualistic everyone is brought up to be self-reliant and be able to fend for themselves. Success in life is dependent on your own capabilities, skills and expertise and you should not necessarily depend on the largesse of others. When we remember that Bristol was from America (an individualistic society) and fundamentally believed in the power of thought, it should come as no surprise that he liked to think of men and women who, like staunch oak trees, can stand firm amid the many crosscurrents of thought that whirl around them.

Although staunchly individualistic, when you read Bristol's book, it is clear that the success he talks of and the examples he uses to demonstrate *The Magic of Believing* usually involve other people. Even Bristol's success wasn't exclusively of his own making. Sure, he thought about becoming rich, but his lucky break was down to the actions of others and especially the army. Belief is one thing, execution is quite another. Implicit within *The Magic of Believing* is recognizing that other people have their part to play in your success. This is where networking comes in. In the past, this required a significant amount of time and effort to keep in touch with the people who could influence your career and help you advance. Today, it is much simpler as there are so many ways in which you can stay connected with those who can help you succeed. Indeed networking is now considered an essential tool to a successful career and if anything has taken on an increased role with the emergence of social media, such as Facebook and Twitter. In a high-tech world, where face-to-face contact is less important than it used to be, ensuring you are networked and 'known' in the market still requires a lot of effort, but this time it can be mostly achieved from behind a screen.

DEFINING IDEA...

'No man is an island, entire of itself; every man is a piece of the continent.'

JOHN DONNE, POET

HERE'S AN IDEA FOR YOU...

How good is your network and how well do you use it? If your network is not as good as it ought to be it would be a good idea to expand it. Why not set up a profile on LinkedIn and start connecting with fellow professionals; it's easier than trying to meet people face to face and is now one of the most effective ways to find work and advance your career.

25 BELIEVING OTHERS

Sometimes it takes someone else to light the fires of success.

When H.G. Wells wrote *The War of the Worlds* in 1898 he had no idea that forty years later it would instil panic across America. When Orson Welles and his Mercury Theatre Players broadcasted their dramatization of Well's book in 1938 the impact was dramatic. People were so convinced that the earth was being invaded by warmongering Martians that they flew into panic; the police were inundated with calls for help, roads were clogged as people escaped the cities and telephone exchanges couldn't cope with the volume of calls. Once people realized that there were neither Martians nor an invasion they returned to their homes, no doubt somewhat embarrassed. Bristol uses the example of *The War of the Worlds* to illustrate how individuals can paint such a convincing image that others will believe it too.

There have been many examples of people in positions of power and influence who have been able to convince others to follow them. The Crusades were set in motion by Pope Innocent II at his speech in Claremont in October 1087. He was able to stir up the emotions of those who were there and create a shared dream that spread across Europe. Kings, knights and the common man were all equally inspired and undertook to march to the Holy Land.

Henry V managed to convince his vastly outnumbered troops at Agincourt in 1415 that they could defeat a French army many times their size. And, a mere few years later Joan of Arc was able to inspire the French to take back everything the English army had won following Agincourt. More recent examples include Martin Luther King and his dream of equality for the African American and John F. Kennedy and his dream of landing the first man on the moon.

We all look to our leaders, who by dint of their position, power, charisma and strength of will are able to inspire us to follow them and do great things. We do so because we share their dreams, as they paint a convincing picture of success and overwhelmingly believe that it is possible to achieve. As Bristol points out, sports events, sales meetings and political rallies all rely on the same principle. They are creating an environment where they arouse the will to win. And from this comes the confidence that will make it possible.

DEFINING IDEA...

'It takes a lot of courage to show your dreams to someone else.'
ERMA BOMBECK, HUMORIST

HERE'S AN IDEA FOR YOU...

The next time you are leading a major project, don't wait until the end to celebrate success, do it at the beginning. When everyone is assembled paint a powerful picture of success and ask everyone to talk about it and what part they will play in making it happen. Not only will it give people the opportunity to meet each other, it will also reinforce the belief that the project will be successful before it even starts.

26 HAVE FAITH

Faith has become associated with belief in God, and often carries negative connotations, like blind trust despite lack of proof. The rational twenty-first century sceptic disregards anything that can't be explained. But it would be a mistake to consider faith to be the preserve of the religious. In fact, as Bristol suggests, we need to place our trust in the seemingly mysterious workings of the subconscious mind and we avoid doing so at our own cost.

Bristol describes our subconscious as a strangely independent part of our minds: one that works unaided by our conscious meddling. Indeed, it works best when our everyday awareness, chewing over mundane concerns or processing data from the senses, is inactive. We like to think we are in charge of our own minds but Bristol points to the considerable influence our silent partner has on our behaviour. A recent experiment found that subjects were more friendly when given a cup of hot coffee to hold than those given an iced coffee. Somehow the temperature influenced social warmth or coolness via subconscious associations. Researchers, at a loss to account for behavioural changes much beyond this tentative explanation, agreed that something was at work that defied traditional investigation.

If the idea of unquestioningly obeying the subconscious is hard to take, consider what it is capable of. It helps in moments of peril, instigating the 'fight or flight' mechanism. If it took a moment to politely bring danger to our conscious attention, it would be too late to act. Similarly it keeps our bodies ticking over and our hearts beating. We unthinkingly trust it with these vital operations, so is faith in it really too much to ask?

Faced with a seemingly impossible decision, we try to muddle through by weighing up the pros and cons of each choice. Should you take the new job and move house for the sake of it or let it go in the hope of finding one, just around the corner, that doesn't require you to uproot your life? Such decisions potentially involve innumerable considerations and we worry that whichever way we choose will end up being the wrong choice. But we also have a feeling in our gut and with time that feeling develops into a conviction. However illogical it may appear considered from the 'outside', we must have faith in this subconscious decision. We may begrudge kowtowing to the subconscious, not knowing the full ins and outs of the decision, but we must work with rather than against it. Bristol emphasizes constant repetition of our goals so that our everyday lives are pointed in that direction; at least we have some control this way. Once we start on this path we have to see it through even when the intuition seems trivial. 'You must continue to believe in the power and wisdom of the subconscious and obediently perform seemingly irrelevant things'. Only with hindsight will you see the logic of the route, says Bristol. Before then you must push onward according to your intuition as though lost in a forest without a map. Only great faith in the ways of the subconscious mind can help us forge such a path into the unknown.

DEFINING IDEA...

'Faith is taking the first step even when you don't see the whole staircase.'
MARTIN LUTHOR KING, JR

HERE'S AN IDEA FOR YOU...

Stumped by a tricky decision? Employ both minds appropriately by first considering the pros and cons of each choice and writing them out in a table. Ask a friend to add their opinions too. With this clear picture achieved, stop worrying about it and go about your day. Within a few days your subconscious will provide you with a strong intuition. Have faith in this decision and work to see it through, confident that it is the right choice.

27 VISUALIZATION

Taking deliberate steps to 'see your success' really works wonders.

Bristol makes a big thing of visualization. In his view, achieving what you want in life requires that you paint a picture of the future you desire in your minds eye. In fact he goes on to state quite unequivocally that, 'without question human imagination or visualization and concentration are the chief factors in developing the magnetic forces of the subconscious mind.' He believed that failure to create and then hold onto a successful mental picture resulted in no action and certainly no accomplishment because your subconscious mind would not be focused on making it a reality. Using visualization techniques is a powerful technique and one that can spur us on to do amazing things. Consider Roger Bannister and the four minute mile.

Before Roger Bannister smashed the four minute mile, conventional wisdom (especially from the medical profession) believed that it was impossible. Indeed doctors at the time thought that anyone who attempted it would die. A ridiculous sentiment now, but back then it really did hold people back from attempting it. Yet Bannister believed it was possible even though there were no models on which to base his belief. So how did he do it? Well, he rehearsed the race over and over again in his mind, feeling, seeing and sensing everything in full Technicolor. When the day came he had the race mapped out in his head and, as we know, he broke the four minute mile. Of course, as soon as this new benchmark had been set a clutch of athletes did exactly the same. Why? Because they were able to drop the limiting belief that had prevented them from running faster than the medics believed was safe.

So what does this tell us? Well, if we want to achieve something that may not have been done before, or even something others have, but we haven't, there is real benefit in applying the same visualization techniques which Bannister did and indeed all other modern athletes and Olympians now do. All this requires us to do is change our attitude, not develop some kind of superhuman ability. So the good news is that it's in everyone's reach. Therefore, just as Bannister was able to practise running the race of his life, you can do exactly the same by visualizing a new job, new house, better relationship and so on. And, as you are in charge of the camera, you can make it as colourful and as memorable as you like.

DEFINING IDEA...

'You're trying to put yourself in that moment and trying to prepare yourself, to have a "memory before the game". I don't know if you'd call it visualizing or dreaming, but I've always done it, my whole life.'
WAYNE ROONEY, FOOTBALLER

HERE'S AN IDEA FOR YOU...

Jot down something you want to achieve. It may be your dream job; a promotion; it might be to ask someone special out for a meal. Then shut your eyes and create a mental image of how you secured the job or promotion, or how you asked the person out. Once created, play it over and over in your mind so that your subconscious can start preparing you for the moment when it arrives

28 THE INVISIBLE HAND

Life moves in mysterious ways, or does it?

Adam Smith came up with the term the invisible hand to describe the self-regulating nature of the markets and as a result has gone down in history as an economic genius. Although Bristol was not writing about the financial markets, the basis of his idea is one that is closely associated with Smith's. Throughout the book he talks of things happening out of the blue to him and others, although he was clear that if you set your mind to something, there would be nothing out of the blue about it. Indeed, as a soldier in World War I, Bristol decided that once he returned to civilian life he would become wealthy, and in his mind it was a decision, not just a wish. Getting to the point where he did become wealthy involved what we would consider a series of disconnected events, but in Bristol's mind demonstrated the power of thought.

Bristol uses his journey from enlisted soldier to investment banker to illustrate the power of his theory. His story starts in 1918 when he arrived in France. Whilst waiting for his service record to catch up with him, he had to live off basic army rations as he would not receive the full pay he was due until his records arrived. It was at this moment, when he had no money, that Bristol set his mind on becoming wealthy. When he enlisted, he stated that his profession was journalism and whilst waiting to be shipped out to France had been training to achieve his commission. Unfortunately, the course was discontinued just after he finished and he arrived in France as an enlisted man, not a commissioned officer. It was shortly after he had made the decision to become wealthy that things started to happen. First he was ordered to see the commanding officer of his battalion where he was given orders to move to First Army Headquarters to run the daily progress bulletin. Over the next few months he kept on thinking about his commission to which he was entitled and then just as he was about to be transferred to the *Stars and Stripes* (the independent US military newspaper, which still operates today) he was offered a commission but chose instead to move to the newspaper given the war was almost over. He eventually made it back to civilian life in 1919. Shortly after arriving back in the United States he was invited to see the president of a well-known club who introduced him to a senior investment banker who subsequently offered him a job. From there Bristol went on to make his fortune and always believed that he did so because of the decision he had made back in 1918. In his mind all the events led to the one outcome he was set on achieving.

DEFINING IDEA...
'Belief creates the actual fact.'
WILLIAM JAMES, US PHILOSOPHER

HERE'S AN IDEA FOR YOU...
Whatever you want from your career or indeed life in general, make a point of believing in it as powerfully as Bristol. Think about it as often as you can and where possible write it down so that your mind remains sharply focused on achieving it.

29 YOU ARE WHAT YOU READ

Bristol brazenly predicts: 'There will never be another business depression if people generally realize that it is with their own fear thoughts that they literally create hard times. They think hard times and hard times follow.' Obviously his message didn't get through.

In 2007 the world started to fall into recession. Banks once said to be 'too big to fail', failed. They panicked and stopped lending. Businesses tightened their belts; people lost their jobs, and with rising unemployment consumption dropped. Before we knew it entire countries were going bankrupt. Ever since, barely a day has passed without the familiar headlines: 'Banks fail', 'long slump', 'negative growth'. We're living through the worst recession since records began, or so we are told. Our financial 'experts' pontificate about something they no longer seem to understand, and we take their word for it. What else can we do?

It seems mad to many of us that this huge system should be allowed to crash and create such misery in the world. As we struggle desperately to regain control of the monster we've created, we only manage to spread more confusion and fear. But we are unanimous about one thing; things are really bad. Politicians and banks give us no reason to doubt it, the media trumpets it and the whole world and its dog is in agreement. Pessimism is winning the day.

This is the power of suggestion at work on a massive scale. Even those who don't understand the situation (and let's be honest, that's most of us), are disheartened by it. A daily diet of no-hope makes us sick with worry. The more we worry, the less we act with confidence and certainty and so the worse it seems to get. Bristol noticed the same outlook working overtime during the Great Depression to the continued detriment of America as a whole. The doom-laden announcements reaching people from the media spread negative emotional thinking that 'became the national chant'.

Clearly negative thinking alone didn't cause the financial crash, but it certainly hasn't helped. The stock market is a bit like life; it responds to both our optimism and our gloom. If we feed this cycle with fearful thoughts we shouldn't really be surprised when it reacts accordingly. To then consume these bad vibrations and let them dictate our outlook, is sheer madness.

Negativity is hard to dodge these days. The 24 hour bad news cycle saps us of the very confidence we need to turn things around. Every morning we digest new terrorism, violence and suffering. We take the views of cheerless commentators as fact and act accordingly, never stopping to question what we consume and how it might affect us. Drummed into us, these views become beliefs. Watered by repetition, such seeds take root in our subconscious and soon they become the guiding principles by which we live our lives.

DEFINING IDEA ...

'I cannot remember the books I've read any more than the meals I have eaten; even so, they have made me.'

RALPH WALDO EMERSON

HERE'S AN IDEA FOR YOU ...

In stark contrast to the recession, the positivity surrounding the London 2012 Olympics seemed to lift the soul of an entire nation, sweeping it up in the jubilant commotion of the media. It was as if the nation had allowed itself a holiday from bad news. Why not take a couple of weeks off reading and watching the news? Give your brain a rest from the misery and see how much (or how little) you miss it.

30 IT'S NOT WHAT YOU SAY, IT'S THE WAY THAT YOU SAY IT

Never forget the power of non-verbal cues.

Bristol places huge emphasis on the subconscious mind and he summarizes its chief powers as intuition, emotion, certitude, inspiration, suggestion, deduction, imagination and organization. Tapping into these qualities was, in his mind, essential to success. As important as these are to us as individuals, Bristol also recognized the power they have on others, especially in relation to convincing others of your intentions, ideas and so on. This is where non-verbal communication comes in.

During the 1984 United States presidential campaign between Ronald Reagan and Walter Mondale, tapes of interviews between the candidates and three news channels, CBS, NBC and ABC were made as part of an experiment. Excerpts were taken from these tapes in which all references to the candidates were removed. These were then shown, with the sound turned off, to a group of randomly chosen people who were asked to score the expressions of the interviewer concerned. The scoring ranged from 1 (extremely negative) to 21 (extremely positive). Whereas two of the interviewers were scored much the same for each candidate (Reagan and Mondale), the ABC interviewer was rated much higher when talking to Reagan. The researchers concluded that this represented a significant bias toward Reagan. This initial finding was followed up to see what impact this had on the voters themselves. The results were profound. In every case where voters had watched the ABC interview, they voted for Reagan in greater numbers than those who had watched either CBS or NBC. It appeared that the facial expressions used by the ABC presenter were enough to influence the electorate to vote for Reagan rather than Mondale. This experiment was repeated in subsequent presidential campaigns with similar results.

The example above illustrates the effect of non-verbal communication and demonstrates why it is so important, especially if you happen to be a presidential candidate. It was Darwin who first recognized the importance of non-verbal communication and since then there has been plenty of research into how it is manifested. According to psychology expert Kendra Cherry, there are eight ways in which we communicate non-verbally: through our facial expression; via our gestures; in the intonation of our voice; our use of body language and posture; how we deploy our personal space; using our gaze; through touch and our appearance (more on that in Idea 50).

It is clear that we are all capable of subconsciously processing the non-verbal cues people give off, whether it be when dating or listening to a CEO speak. It makes sense to master it.

DEFINING IDEA ...

'The most important thing in communication is to hear what isn't being said.'

PETER F. DRUCKER, MANAGEMENT GURU

HERE'S AN IDEA FOR YOU ...

Whenever you communicate consider how you are delivering the message, not just the content of the message itself. It doesn't matter if this is a presentation to senior management or an appraisal meeting, think carefully about your body language and the non-verbal cues you are giving off. Do your best to ensure they are congruent.

31 THE MYSTERIOUS MAGNETISM OF POSITIVITY

Bristol suggests that if you follow his instruction to the letter, and successfully plant an idea in your subconscious through constant reaffirmation of your goal, your subconscious will work its 'magic'. He stops short of properly explaining this, relying instead on mystical insinuation. But there is a more realistic way of understanding it.

There are a few passages in *The Magic of Believing* that are memorable for all the wrong reasons. Even the most open-minded of us would have to question Bristol's accounts of the experiences of some positive-minded people; people who always find parking spaces because they sincerely believe they will. One woman ignores the advice of her mechanic and takes a long road trip even though her tyres are dangerously worn. She completes the journey unscathed thanks, asserts Bristol, to her strength of mind and determination. We might say she was just lucky, but we shouldn't entirely discard the power of the mind.

Bristol's system works like a self-perpetuating machine. Positivity feeds on positivity, making the planting of self-confident beliefs easier, and counteracting any negative thoughts. This is a familiar notion in the self-help tradition; it is the Law of Attraction or the Secret. This connectivity between positive outlook and results often convinces otherwise rational people that 'mind power' can influence events. But if we consider what happens to our outlook when we are in a positive frame of mind it is easier to explain. On a good day the sun is shining, the birds are singing and all seems right with the world. Everything seems to be in our favour, from the traffic lights on the way to work to grabbing the last doughnut in the canteen. Sure, 'negative' things happen but for some reason they don't register or don't bother us. Compare this with a bad day. You wake up on the wrong side, you miss the bus and you have to work late. It's very hard to see the positive, no matter how hard you try. The fact is the birds are still singing and the sun is still shining, but we don't notice them.

The mental outlook you start out with affects how you see the world. Both negative and positive frames of mind seem to attract their like because they colour how we consider our experiences. Bristol is asking that we wholeheartedly cultivate a positivity that begets itself. From this perspective we might look back on strange coincidences and see some sort of logic to them, but this is only positive hindsight working in our favour. The real explanation is that, in choosing a positive outlook from the start, we both set our expectations and define how we will react to events. Once experienced this can become a self-fulfilling mental habit that drastically changes our way of life.

DEFINING IDEA...

'If you see the world and yourself through a lens smudged by negativity then you'll find much misery. If you look outwards and inwards through a lens brightened by positivity you'll find much to be happy and appreciative about.'

HENRIK EDBERG, **THE 7 TIMELESS HABITS OF HAPPINESS**

HERE'S AN IDEA FOR YOU...

If you're having a bad day, stop dwelling on it and instead write a list of the things you are grateful for. Allow yourself to recognize the things you might normally take for granted: your friends and family, the food on your table, the roof over your head. Cultivating a grateful attitude may help to kick start a positive outlook that will favourably affect the rest of your day.

32 REGRETS ... I HAVE A FEW

Most people regret things they haven't done, which seems pointless.

The empowering thing about *The Magic of Believing* is that it forces you to think carefully about and ultimately discard those patterns of thinking and behaviour that inhibit your ability to realize your full potential. We all have them: the inner voice; the nagging doubts; fear of failure, and so on. Although many of these could be considered legitimate and hence worth consuming energy over, there is one pattern of thinking that adds no value at all and that's regret.

Regrets are funny things as, in the main, they are associated with things we haven't done rather than those we have. A recent survey by the British Heart Foundation confirmed this. According to the survey, people spend two hours a week ruminating over their regrets. Taken over a lifetime this means that the average person spends over a year focused on such things. Clearly if you have actually done something that was considered wrong, such as say hurt someone for example, then feeling some kind of remorse is probably right, but in the majority of cases, we seem to spend most of our energy regretting things we haven't done or not done enough of. The survey highlighted people's chief regrets, which included such gems as: not travelling more; not eating healthily; not keeping in touch with friends; not saving enough money; being lazy at school and so on. What is fascinating about this list is that each regret seems somewhat passive and, to be honest, weak. As one pundit in a newspaper article quite rightly pointed out, if you want to travel more, get yourself a passport and book a holiday and if you really want to keep in touch with friends, pick up the phone, jump onto Facebook or send them an email. How hard can that be?

It appears that if we spend two hours a week worrying about our regrets, then on some level we must like it, otherwise why do it? Perhaps in the end, regrets are really a socially acceptable way of expressing our excuses for not doing things we would like to or feel that we should. They allow us to eat unhealthily, stay at home rather than travel, not bother with our studies and fail to pick up the phone to our friends. They allow us to sleepwalk through our lives and provide the ready made excuses why we have not achieved what we would have really liked to. If we spent less time focused on our regrets and more time on positive action, who knows what we could achieve. Letting regrets get in the way of progress is, in the end, inexcusable.

DEFINING IDEA…

'I'd rather regret doing something than not doing something.'
JAMES HETFIELD, LEAD SINGER OF METALLICA

HERE'S AN IDEA FOR YOU…

Do you have any regrets? If so, try this. List them on a piece of paper and turn each regret into a positive commitment. For example, if you have written 'I regret not eating healthily', rewrite the statement as 'I will eat a balanced diet'. Once you have finished your list why not break your resolutions down into specific actions?

33 THE MIRROR TECHNIQUE

Bristol presents the mirror technique as an ideal way to engage the power of the subconscious. Practice makes perfect, goes the saying, and this can be applied to cultivating inner strength and drive. 'Within a few days you will have developed a sense of confidence that you never realized you could build within yourself', says Bristol.

Bristol recommends this technique as a particularly effective way to root your desire in your subconscious so that the 'magic' process of achieving it can begin. Look at yourself in the mirror and tell yourself, out loud and with gusto, that you will achieve your goal. In this self-encounter you 'play' both yourself and your imagined audience, with a twofold benefit. Firstly, you will see yourself as others do, allowing you to recognize and improve on the overall impression that your demeanour gives off. Many career centres offer a similar opportunity: practice interviews are recorded, allowing the applicant to witness her performance, nervous tics and all, and then work to iron them out. Videoing yourself is probably a better idea than addressing the mirror; it creates a genuine sensation of being watched and, with playback, allows you to analyse different aspects of your performance separately.

This opportunity for self-analysis feeds into the second benefit, which is that, through repetition of the technique, you start to build a healthy foundation of confidence. 'Look into the very depths of your eyes', encourages Bristol. 'Breathe deeply ... until you feel a sense of power, strength, and determination'. The technique is about engaging with your desire on a more intense level, bringing your intangible 'mind stuff' out into the real world and turning confidence into a palpable experience. You should 'make a regular ritual of it' every morning. Frequently bearing witness to your expressed determination will help you to cultivate a foundation level of self-worth and confidence. You can then build on this throughout the day, calling on this inner strength to help you face its challenges.

According to popular myth, Winston Churchill would never make a public speech without first practising it in front of a mirror, and he is rightly regarded as one of the most influential orators of the twentieth century. The 'imagine your audience naked' technique is also often (probably erroneously) attributed to the war-time prime minister, although this is far less widely recommended. Bristol isn't so much interested in calming your nerves with whimsical thought experiments. Instead, the mirror technique steps up the practice of mental picturing, developing it into a sensation of greater clarity and purpose. If wholeheartedly practised, it should afford you a very real boost in confidence. More importantly, repeated affirmations in front of the mirror will more readily embed your goals into the subconscious mind, setting the necessary groundwork for the process that leads to their achievement.

DEFINING IDEA...

'To convince others, first you must convince yourself'

ANONYMOUS

HERE'S AN IDEA FOR YOU...

Try combining the mirror and card techniques. Stand with a confident posture in front of a video camera. Read out your prepared mind-prompt cards, working to convince yourself of your own determination. Familiarize yourself with that feeling as often as possible; leave cards on your desk at work or play back the video last thing at night to reinvigorate your drive.

34 SCRUPULOUS OPTIMISM

Having an optimistic outlook is central to success.

One of the many things that stand out from *The Magic of Believing* is how important having a positive outlook is to success. Setting your mind on something that you really want, as Bristol did back in 1918 when he decided to be wealthy, is of course important, but so is maintaining a positive outlook. Without this it is difficult to deal with the inevitable setbacks that occur when undertaking any significant endeavour. Positive thinking necessitates that we have an optimistic outlook and ideally one which is scrupulous.

Much has been written about optimism and pessimism and although pessimism is often given a hard press, a positive outlook requires a mix of both. Roger Scruton an English philosopher, writer and composer has written an excellent book, *The Uses of Pessimism and the Dangers of False Hope*. This sets out the value of what Scruton terms the Scrupulous Optimist. The Scrupulous Optimist is someone who possesses the desire to drive things forward but also takes into account the pessimist's view and considers the downsides and constraints. In his mind, to be truly successful you need both perspectives to work in concert. The Scrupulous Optimist can trump what Scruton terms the Unscrupulous Optimist. Unscrupulous Optimists see no downside and typically dismiss the value in reviewing and assessing the potential downsides of an endeavour. As a result they are rarely successful.

The importance of this is illustrated by the Boeing Dreamliner (787) project. The aircraft, now in production, is one of the two largest planes in the world, the other being the Airbus A380. Both are ground breaking in terms of their size and their green credentials and both compete head-to-head in the highly competitive aviation market. Although the Boeing 787 had a difficult birth, it was the belief in the end vision that kept the project running despite the significant delays and cost overruns. Launching the project in 2003, Boeing had originally planned for the first flight to take place in August 2007. However, problems in procurement, software systems, component design and the supply chain led to a series of delays that continued for almost four years. As delay followed delay, Boeing decided to suspend any further announcements until everything came right and the plane was ready to fly. The 787 was finally certified in August 2011, almost four years late. Boeing's belief in the project was always unwavering even though it led to multibillion dollar write-offs and significant cost escalations. But this belief was not blindly optimistic; it was more along the lines of Scruton's scrupulous optimism. They knew that the project was never going to be simple and as such they were willing to deal with the inevitable setbacks whilst holding onto the vision of producing one of the most advanced airliners in the world.

DEFINING IDEA...

'Success is a lousy teacher. It seduces smart people into thinking they can't lose.'

BILL GATES

HERE'S AN IDEA FOR YOU...

The next time you set yourself a major objective, take the advice of Scruton and view it through the eyes of a scrupulous optimist. As well as writing down the objective take the trouble to think about those things that could get in the way of the achievement.

35 THINKING BIG TO BE BIG

Thinking big can lead to big dividends.

There is something unique about the famous, especially Hollywood film stars and those who have reached the heights of the music business; it's almost as if they were destined to become famous from birth. Such people, according to research, are wired differently. Unlike those who may have become famous through other means such as Nobel Prize winners or Olympic medal winners they have an enduring quality to their fame. This aspect is down to them making fame a singular goal in their life – fame for fame's sake, you might say. Whereas the fame of the scientist or world-class athlete is down to a combination of hard work and luck, the biggest stars make their own luck.

Irrespective of whether such people are wired differently, what is interesting about them is that they assume greatness and are treated accordingly; they may lack the humility of the Olympian or scientist, but they expect to be, and usually are, treated differently. Lady GaGa is a good case in point. Born into an Italian family in New York she dropped out of university to pursue her dream of becoming famous. She is a proudly aggressive seeker of pop culture celebrity inspired by glam rock, in particular by David Bowie and Queen. Her belief in becoming famous was achieved through her 2008 debut album, *The Fame*. Since then she has courted attention as any celebrity has to; once it's achieved, they never want to lose it and fall back into a world of obscurity.

This notion of taking on the mantle of greatness chimes well with the following extract from Bristol's book: 'There are many women who have improved their appearance by continuing to feel the delights of beauty, by thinking thoughts of the beautiful, by wearing stylish clothes, by adding things of beauty to their surroundings, by developing poise and easy carriage and by constantly telling themselves that they are going to win out'. What he means here is that by thinking big, beautiful, successful, or whatever it may be, you will begin to behave in that way and ultimately become what it is that you want to be. What's more, people around you will be convinced that you are too and begin to treat you in a way that is congruent with your behaviour. Let's face it, apart from a modicum of talent, most film and pop stars are really not much different from you or me. The fundamental difference is that they believe they are as good as, if not better than, their own press.

DEFINING IDEA...

'Think little goals and expect little achievements. Think big goals and win big success.'

DAVID JOSEPH SCHWARTZ, AMERICAN BUSINESSMAN

HERE'S AN IDEA FOR YOU...

Assuming that you don't want to be famous like Lady GaGa, but do want to deploy some of the self-confidence that she displays, what can you do? The best way is to take the advice of Bristol and consider how you can both create and reinforce the image of confidence and greatness. Think about your clothes, pay attention to your posture, work on your language.

36 BREAKING CONVENTION

To be successful, we sometimes need to break convention.

When Roger Bannister smashed the four minute mile (see Idea 27) he broke the convention at the time which stated that no one could run that fast without killing themselves. Although Bristol didn't mention the breaking of convention specifically, he alluded to it in many of his examples. When discussing the power of repeated suggestion Bristol highlighted the example of the belief that tomatoes were poisonous until someone ate one and didn't die. Until that point everyone believed the received wisdom that tomatoes were bad for you and didn't eat them; afterwards people ate them without a second's thought. Such is the power of convention. Conventions and paradigms are all around us and although they can help us navigate through our lives by setting boundaries to what we can and cannot do, sometimes they are incorrect or outdated and believing in them can limit our success. To be successful therefore requires that we sometimes have to break convention, although to do so can be difficult and usually takes courage. For example, although Copernicus realized that the earth revolved around the sun, he was unwilling to overturn the convention of the time that the earth was at the centre of our planetary system. However, Galileo was willing to challenge this convention and as a result suffered at the hands of the Roman Inquisition and spent the rest of his life under house arrest.

The history of inoculation is a prime example of the value of breaking convention. In 1721 there was an outbreak of smallpox in Boston which came from those aboard HMS Seahorse. The usual reaction to such periodic endemics was to accept it as divine judgement with the only response being to escape the city and head for the countryside. On this occasion one man thought differently, Cotton Mather. He wrote the following in his diary: 'The practice of conveying and suffering the Smallpox has never been used in America, or indeed in our Nation, but how many lives might be saved by it if were practised?' Using the power of the church, Mather was able to push through a scientific innovation in the face of strong opposition from none other than the medical profession. The results thankfully spoke for themselves. Of the 248 people who were inoculated during the outbreak, only six died, whilst by comparison 844 people died of the 5,980 people who contracted the disease but were not inoculated. As when anyone challenges convention, there were those who took umbrage – a primitive grenade was thrown through a window of Mather's house with the following message, 'COTTON MATHER, You Dog, Dam you. I'll inoculate you with this, with a Pox to you.' Mather's innovation set in motion work that resulted in Edward Jenner's breakthrough with cowpox and vaccination, something we should all be thankful for.

DEFINING IDEA...

'You don't learn to walk by following rules. You learn by doing, and by falling over.'

RICHARD BRANSON

HERE'S AN IDEA FOR YOU...

Think about the conventions which frame your life. Do any of these hold you back from achieving your goals? Consider their validity and whether they are just repeated suggestions and something to be challenged. Determine how you can break them in order to achieve your goals.

37 CAN-DO CULTURE

'Everyone is a creation of themselves', asserts Bristol 'and what is a big business, a village, a city, a nation but merely a collection of individual humans controlling and operating it with their thinking and believing?' If a can-do attitude can lead to remarkable achievements in the individual's life, just think what it could do if everyone embraced Bristol's ideas.

The power of repetition and affirmation can set the subconscious into action and produce profound effects on the way we live. But what is the potential of this power of belief on a wider scale? If we consider the families we belong to, the organizations we work for, the societies we live in, we can see how much of our daily lives involve interacting with groups. Our lives are inextricably tied up with the lives of others and what unites them all is a set of common values or beliefs. You might wonder how on earth you came to be sharing an office with certain people, but think for a moment and you will easily uncover the fundamental beliefs that unite you. These may be simple things like the sincere belief in the work you're doing or the value of the product you're selling or they may be more deeply held convictions about the purpose and meaning of your lives.

In *The Magic of Believing* Bristol reveals the power of the central idea, instilled in people by repetition, to be the secret of the great movements of history. His examples largely highlight abuse of this power in politics and religion; the mass hypnosis of nations under powerful leaders like Hitler or the brainwashing of devotees by cult figureheads. Belief can be dangerous in such hands, but with positive application the theory can achieve great results. Everyone knows the fable of the two donkeys tethered to one another and pulling desperately in opposite directions, neither getting anywhere. Many organizations do the same thing without knowing it. The motivations and values of its management and staff pull this way and that because the core values of the company have gone undefined or have been lost somewhere along the way. Such behaviour not only trips the organization up, it also drives away clients who pick up on the implicit confusion in the company.

These days organizations produce entire books on their corporate culture. It's possible to go too far in this direction and reduce the key message to empty business-speak, but successful businesses usually have strong core values that have become ingrained through their repetition and affirmation in the workplace – on posters, in meetings, in emails and in customer-facing material. Far from being brainwashed, says Bristol, the individual comes to understand and associate with such values 'heart and soul', allowing beliefs to penetrate into the subconscious and become real for them. Once it's reached the subconscious, he asserts, it's only a matter of time before positive action based on the founding belief becomes spontaneous and moves the whole company in the right direction.

DEFINING IDEA

'If everyone is moving forward together, then success takes care of itself.'
HENRY FORD

HERE'S AN IDEA FOR YOU...

If your daily work activity feels a little too much like the daily grind, gather your colleagues together and have each member offer their thoughts on the value and purpose of their work to the client, to the organization and to them personally. Draw up a brief manifesto detailing the values of the team and display it prominently throughout the office as a reminder to inspire even the smallest tasks with the big-picture significance of the work the company does.

38 KNOW THYSELF

If you met yourself in the future, what would you think?

Bristol is someone who took a lot of interest in other people. He spent years interviewing and studying the attributes that made those he investigated successful. And it was this process, together with his extensive research into, amongst other things, psychology and metaphysics that allowed him to develop the kernel of the ideas in *The Magic of Believing*. What is interesting however is that Bristol appeared not to delve into himself that much, or at least he never mentioned it in his book.

As you read the book, what is clear is that in order to be successful and indeed to commit to the ideas that Bristol writes about, you need to know yourself and what really makes you tick. Many of us fail to pursue our dreams and ambitions because other factors get in the way – self-limiting beliefs, the criticism of others and the fear of failure to name but a few. If only we ditched such behaviours we could achieve whatever we wanted; simple to say but actually much harder to do in practice. Although difficult, *The Magic of Believing* requires that you understand yourself to a sufficient degree that you are able to truly believe in your personal success, targets or however you frame your future.

Plato's 'know thyself' is a good watchword and something to aspire to; knowing what makes you who you are and what drives your thoughts, feelings and behaviours is fundamental to your success. It is also central to understanding how others perceive you, which is equally important. Figuring out what drives you can be achieved in a multitude of ways.

There are plenty of online personality assessments which you can take which help you figure out how you view the world around you, what your key behavioural traits are and so on. There is also coaching, which can be as deep as you need it to be and even though some may drift into the realms of therapy, it is a great way to really get to the nub of who you are – your core beliefs if you like. Once you have done this it will be much easier to get congruence between your life goals and your actions and it will bring *The Magic of Believing* to life.

One recent thing some newspapers have been doing is to interview people of note and ask them what their 18-year-old self would think. It is fascinating to see so many of them state that the 18 year old would be amazed at what they have achieved, and that they're safe in the knowledge that they followed their dreams.

DEFINING IDEA...

'He who knows others is wise; he who knows himself is enlightened.'

LAO TZU, TAOIST SAGE

HERE'S AN IDEA FOR YOU...

Commit to doing a couple of online personality assessments. There are a lot to choose from, but particularly good are the 'whole brain dominance', DISC, Belbin and Myers & Briggs assessments. Each provides a slightly different perspective and if you take them all you will gain a rounded and pretty comprehensive perspective on who you are.

39 SMILE AND THE WHOLE WORLD SMILES WITH YOU

How people react to us is a product of how we present ourselves.

It is said that as married couples grow older together they begin to look the same. Fanciful though this may sound, it does have some scientific basis. Whereas newlywed couples typically bear no resemblance to each other, after twenty-five years of marriage there are subtle similarities. Studies which involve people matching photos of married couples, both newlywed and after twenty-five years of marriage, resulted in the older couples being matched more often and more consistently than the newlyweds. The belief is that the facial similarity is the result of decades of shared emotions, which bring the same muscles into play. In addition, married couples often unconsciously mimic the facial expressions of their spouses in silent empathy over the years they are together.

This subtle matching and mirroring of our expressions can be interpreted more broadly as people will react to our outward appearance when we meet them. And our outward appearance is a factor of our thoughts about the person we are interacting with. This is an observation that Bristol made when he reflected on someone who had taken a violent dislike to him. Bristol believed that some of our enemies may be of our own making and that both friends and enemies are merely a reflection of our own thoughts – the other fellow will consider us an enemy or a friend entirely based on the picture which we ourselves conjure up. So as the adage goes, smile and the whole world smiles with you.

This can be taken a stage further by using a technique known as matching and mirroring. This involves matching another person's non-verbal communication, expressed through their body language, and developing a simple rhythm in which you are able to follow their cues and build rapport and, ultimately, gain their trust. The process of matching and mirroring extends to body movements (hands, legs, facial expressions, and so on), tonal quality of the voice (high, low, loud and quiet) and breathing. So, if the person crosses their legs, is breathing slowly and has a quiet voice, so should you. And as they move their arms or legs, or raise their voice you should follow. After a while, you can even test if you have developed a rhythm by seeing if they follow your lead when you do something subtle such as moving your watch strap. When matching and mirroring is combined with a positive mind set about the other person, it can be a powerful way to develop a positive relationship with them. It can also be a superb way to win over a perceived (or real) enemy.

DEFINING IDEA...

'Behaviour is a mirror in which everyone displays his own image.'
JOHANN WOLFGANG VON GOETHE

HERE'S AN IDEA FOR YOU...

Think about how you could use matching and mirroring at work. Why not start by practising with your spouse or a close friend so that you get used to how to apply it. When you are comfortable introduce it the work setting, such as in one-to-one meetings – don't forget to take a positive view of the person you are with.

40 FROM THE FRINGE

The ideas and concepts we take for granted were once considered radical.

Watching old science fiction films is always interesting because what used to constitute science fiction say 20 or 30 years ago is now science fact or even, in some cases, yesterday's news. Old movies that show people communicating via mobile devices or using computers or other technical gadgets seem very passé today. Although we haven't got to the point where we can travel across time, there is talk of a manned flight to Mars. What this tells us is that what might seem fantastical or indeed radical often becomes part of everyday life at a later date. Before the mid-twentieth century the idea of space flight was seen as a radical concept and something that only Dan Dare or Captain Kirk could do but then, in 1961, the Soviets sent Yuri Gagarin into the Earth's orbit.

The journey from the radical fringe to part of the establishment can be a difficult and uncomfortable one, however. When Bristol first revealed his ideas he was met by scepticism and more often than not derision, but he still persevered because he believed there was something fundamental in the power of thought. His ideas were considered radical at the time, which explains the reactions he got, but over time they have been more broadly accepted. Such things as neurolinguistic programming and Functional Magnetic Resonance Imaging devices that are able to measure brain activity have both added credibility to his ideas. We still know so little about the functioning of the brain, and yet the more we discover, the more powerful it seems. Bristol saw the reactions he received as a paradox: 'Many apparently well-educated men and women in their respective fields, will, in their broad ignorance, condemn the idea of thought power and will make no endeavour to learn about it; and yet, every one of them, if successful, has unconsciously made use of it ... Countless men whose ideas developed the very civilization in which we live today have been hooted at, slandered, and even crucified by the ignoramuses of their times.' Strong stuff indeed, but certainly true. There are many examples throughout history of those who had ideas which were initially lambasted until the evidence was overwhelming. For example, Carlos Finlay, the French-Scottish doctor who discovered that Yellow Fever was transmitted by mosquitoes, was written off as a crank until an army physician stationed in India provided irrefutable evidence that Finlay was correct. So often it seems, great ideas and advances come in from the fringe. We just need to give them time to develop and perhaps give their authors less of a hard ride.

DEFINING IDEA...

'I think there is a world market for about five computers'

THOMAS J. WATSON, CHAIRMAN OF THE BOARD OF IBM

HERE'S AN IDEA FOR YOU...

Think about how open minded you are. Are you someone who embraces new ideas and concepts, or dismisses them because they appear radical or out of line with convention? To help you become more open minded, read widely.

41 WHAT DO YOU WANT?

'Most people have a general idea that they would like to be a success, but beyond that everything is vague,' says Bristol, observing that many people become little more than victims of the influences that pull them this way and that. If you ever hope to be an achiever 'it is vital that you know exactly what you want out of life.'

In Douglas Adams' sci-fi epic, *The Hitchhiker's Guide to the Galaxy*, a vast, sentient computer called Deep Thought is asked to solve the ultimate question. For time immemorial mankind has struggled with the question of 'Life, the Universe … Everything!' Finally an answer is in sight. It'll take some time, admits Deep Thought, somewhere in the region of seven and a half million years. Aeons pass and finally the great day arrives. You're not going to like it, admits a sheepish Deep Thought to the descendents of the original programmers. The answer is 42. It turns out that the ultimate question itself was insufficiently defined. With an unknown question, how can there be a meaningful answer?

In *The Magic of Believing* Bristol makes it clear that the first step towards our goals must be as sure footed as the following steps, if not more so. This first step defines your purpose, laying the foundations on which future success depends. You must know what it is you are aiming for. If you don't know, how can you even move forward? By knowing, Bristol means having so clear an idea of what you want that you can picture it fully and imagine yourself achieving it. This is all part of the picturing technique, one of Bristol's key exercises for getting your subconscious working.

Once pictured your desire becomes a conviction that is reinforced by constant repetition and affirmation. With time you believe wholeheartedly in the inevitability of the achievement and your subconscious gives you the power to work ceaselessly towards it. It is the development of a sort of faith that you will achieve your goal, helping you persevere through moments of doubt. Perseverance would be impossible without a clear end in mind. An end that is fixed and vivid is by definition more achievable than a wishy-washy hope that something-or-other will work out. Yet this is what many of us do. We act as if we're frightened to make a decision one way or another. According to Bristol, all it takes is a decisive determination earned from finally deciding and declaring our purpose to give us the necessary propulsion to get us going on the right track.

Following the fairly disastrous initial set back, Adams' programmers produce a planet-sized computer to formulate the Ultimate Question. The planet in question is the planet Earth, and the question is believed to be hidden somewhere within the subconscious of human beings. This is a liberating re-affirmation of our existential freedom: it's up to us to define our destinies, and it all begins when we take up the challenge and define the purpose of our own lives.

DEFINING IDEA...

'If you don't know where you are going, you'll probably end up somewhere else.'

LEWIS CARROLL

HERE'S AN IDEA FOR YOU...

What did you want to be when you were at school? Before the responsibilities of life deadened our ambitions, our options seemed unlimited. Did you get to where you wanted to be? If not, imagine yourself free from the cares of the world and list five things you want to gain or accomplish in your life. You'll never get anywhere unless you know where you're going.

42 THE CARD TECHNIQUE

'The person with a fixed goal always before him, causes it, through repetition to be buried deeply in his subconscious,' asserts Bristol. 'Just pursue the thought unceasingly'. To aid this, Bristol recommends his card technique. The idea is to arrange to regularly prompt your mind into visualizing your goal several times a day. Doing so will effectively root the desire within your subconscious and keep your purpose and resolve steady.

Once you have defined and visualized your goal, assign a couple of words to it that help you easily conjure it in your mind's eye. Write these words on several cards and stick them up around your home, your place of work, anywhere that is likely to catch your eye on a regular basis. Hide some in your wallet, your bag, your jacket pockets so that you stumble upon them randomly during the day. Bristol suggests sticking one at the foot of your bed so that the last thing in your mind is the visualization of your desire. Sleep is a chance for your subconscious mind to chew over the problems you give it (see Idea 5). On waking up, with your mind fresh and receptive, the seed will be planted once again, helping you to go about your day with a continuity of focus and to work with whatever intuitions are produced by your subconscious.

To some extent the card technique is basic self-motivation. Since you are what you read (see Idea 29) some conveniently placed prompts can refocus the mind and might change the course of otherwise directionless days. But the function of the cards is more than this. It ties in with

Bristol's insistence of the need for repetition. It is through constantly reminding ourselves of our purpose and working our way to achieving it bit by bit that our desires can be realized.

The theory behind this idea might seem obvious, but we probably won't realize the truth of it until we try. You might feel self-conscious leaving little messages to yourself, but consider advertising: your mind consumes other people's messages all the time. Their message is invariably 'without this you're nothing – so get it now!' You might like to think you're not naïve enough to fall for it. Yet how often do you pick the brand you know over the one you don't? It's all too easy to bring to mind the tagline of your favourite products. Why? Because advertising works; if it didn't, organizations wouldn't spend millions a year on it and subliminal advertising wouldn't be such a controversial topic. Bristol is merely suggesting that we use the power of advertising, of subliminally prompting our subconscious minds, to our advantage. Every time we read a card the mental image will pop up in our mind's eye before sinking back into the subconscious again to be worked on anew.

DEFINING IDEA...

'Visualize this thing that you want, see it, feel it, believe in it. Make your mental blue print, and begin to build.'
ROBERT COLLIER, SELF-HELP AUTHOR

HERE'S AN IDEA FOR YOU...

Buy post-its or business cards for your mental prompts and stick them up around your home. Better still, develop mini posters on a computer or frame inspiring quotes or images to better work on your mind. Don't let it become stale – move your prompts around regularly to keep them fresh and effective in drawing your attention and implanting their messages deep into your subconscious.

43 THE POWER OF DESIRE

If you want something badly enough, you can overcome any obstacle.

Partnerships are interesting places to work. They are both highly political and very competitive and a place where you sink or swim. They also demonstrate one of the key tenets from Bristol's book – the power of desire. As he says in *The Magic of Believing*, 'Another important point is that one essential to success is that your desire be an all-encompassing one, your thoughts and aims to be co-ordinated, and your energy be concentrated and applied without let-up.'

You can often spot those who will make partner from the first time you meet them. Such people have an incredibly strong desire to make it to that level. Everything they do is designed to achieve that objective and everything that comes with it, the kudos, the cash and the title. This often requires them to make enormous sacrifices, navigate the often byzantine political landscape and climb over everyone else to get there. Nothing is allowed to get in their way. It should come as no surprise that most of them make it. There are also those who like the idea of partner, but lack the burning desire to make it happen; they rarely make it. Even from this simple example, it is possible to see that desire lies at the heart of getting what you want out of life, whatever it is.

Although *The Magic of Believing* places a strong emphasis on desire it misses one key component that is essential to success and that is congruence. As the partnership example highlighted, those who lack the burning desire are unlikely to make partner because there is a lack of congruence between what they do and what they really want. Take Mike Tyson and Mohammed Ali. Both became world champion boxers but both had very different desires even though the outcome may have been the same. Mike Tyson's goal wasn't to become a champion boxer per se, but to provide for his wife and children and to be financially secure. He could have achieved the objective in many different ways, but succeeded through his boxing. Many years later when he tried a comeback he failed to reclaim his crown as he didn't have those desires behind becoming a world champion boxer any more. He summed this up by saying 'I lost my desire, I'm not hungry anymore. I'm wealthy, my kids have money, I have nothing to fight for.' Ali's goal and desire was always to be a champion boxer. His objective was fame and he achieved it and even though he was never the world's greatest boxer, we all remember him.

DEFINING IDEA...

'The will to win, the desire to succeed, the urge to reach your full potential … these are the keys that will unlock the door to personal excellence.'
CONFUCIUS

HERE'S AN IDEA FOR YOU...

Consider what you want out of life and then think about how much you desire it. If it is strong enough it is likely that you will achieve it. But, if your desire is not as strong as it ought to be (be honest with yourself), then it might be that you need to reassess what your goals are.

44 HAVING THE COURAGE OF YOUR CONVICTIONS

Sometimes achieving our goals requires that we overcome our fears.

One of the major influences on Bristol as he developed his ideas was organized religion. He was intrigued by the way it was able to hold such a powerful sway over people. Most religions rely on having faith in a god who, although invisible, controls the word around us and to achieve this they must cultivate a powerful sense of conviction in their followers. Bristol could see the power that such conviction has on people, but he also observed instances where it was not particularly strong: 'However, I am forced to the conclusion that many people go through the lip-service act of saying their prayers without the slightest belief that those prayers will be answered. Consequently, they are not answered.' Conviction therefore is central to *The Magic of Believing*. With conviction comes the need to follow through or as it is often put, having the courage of your convictions. And with courage comes the need to overcome the inevitable fears that come with any major undertaking; fear of failure being the most significant. Nicola Philips is an expert on the management of fear in and outside of the workplace and in her book *Fear Without Loathing*, she states that more than anything, it is our fears that keep us stuck in places we don't want to be. She believes that in order to overcome our fears we must better understand them, be willing to accept them, but very importantly not lose, or overcome them. This goes against our natural inclination to avoid or control our fears, but from her perspective is a much more healthy response. She identifies seven fears – beginning, fear, disappointment, success, choice, unworthiness and ending, each of which she explores in some detail, so the book is well worth the read. One of the key points she makes, which is especially pertinent to Bristol's ideas, is that fear is so closely linked to desire that when you defend against one, you inevitably defend against the other.

Winston Churchill is a perfect example of someone who had the courage of his convictions. During the 1930s, Churchill took the lead in warning the country of the threat posed by Germany and advocated rearmament. When war finally arrived in September 1939, he was first appointed First Lord of the Admiralty and, following the resignation of Neville Chamberlain, prime minister. He is best remembered for his steadfast refusal to capitulate in the face of the German threat, especially after the fall of France in 1940 when Britain stood alone against the Nazi threat. His speeches and radio broadcasts helped inspire the British people to fight and eventually defeat the Germans. Like most people, however, Churchill had his fears and he battled against depression throughout his life.

DEFINING IDEA...

'All the strength and force of man comes from his faith in things unseen. He who believes is strong; he who doubts is weak. Strong convictions precede great actions.'

JAMES FREEMAN CLARKE, AMERICAN CLERGYMAN

HERE'S AN IDEA FOR YOU...

Take some time to reflect on your fears. Write them down and consider how they hold you back and what you can do to embrace them rather than control or avoid them. Consider how adjusting your understanding of your fears could help you achieve your goals.

45 ME ... A CHIEF EXECUTIVE?

'How few, working day after day, ever realize that it is within their own power to sit someday in the executive's place and give orders?' asks Bristol. He asserts that we all have the ability to be a chief executive ... it's just a question of mind set.

If there is one common theme that runs through Bristol's book it is the power of self-belief. Not just in the positive sense, as limiting beliefs can be just as powerful as those which are optimistic. Pretty much all models of success are predicated on believing that you can do anything and focus heavily on overcoming the feelings, beliefs and self-imposed constraints that prevent us from realizing our potential. There are plenty of examples of people doing the seemingly impossible. Take Felix Baumgartner who, on 14 October 2012, became the first man to break the sound barrier without any form of engine power. Having ascended in a capsule to 24 miles above the earth's surface, he jumped out, freefalling back to earth at a speed of 1,342.8 km/h (834.4 mph). He almost certainly had his doubts and concerns but he overcame these to make it into the record books.

Although there may be very few people who want to jump out of balloons on the edge of space, there are certainly many more who would like to rise up to the senior ranks of an organization. Many people believe they will never achieve this, or indeed feel they are incapable of making it to senior positions in companies, and yet even the most powerful of chief executives started at the bottom. Bristol believed the failure of people to reach the top was more a question of mind set than anything else. As he says, 'Many employees hold to the idea that their work is given to them merely that they may further the interests of their employers. They never entertain the thought that they are actually working for themselves, the employer merely furnishing the tools and the place for the employee to work.' In Bristol's mind anyone has the ability to become a chief executive, but to do so means shaking off the limiting beliefs that prevent us from getting there. Of course, there is a bit more to this than meets the eye. Research has highlighted the common factors associated with many chief executives: years of hard work, getting a good education, and gaining extensive experience, often by starting at a low position in an organization. But what is also clear is that most successful business people are made, not born. What we can take away from this is that if you believe you can be a chief executive and want it enough, you can get there. It boils down to Bristol's key tenet – self-belief.

DEFINING IDEA...

'Most success springs from an obstacle or failure. I became a cartoonist largely because I failed in my goal of becoming a successful executive.'
SCOTT ADAMS, CREATOR OF DILBERT

HERE'S AN IDEA FOR YOU...

Consider whether your mind set holds you back from realizing your ambitions at work. Capture any limiting beliefs you might have and think about whether these are legitimate or an outdated way of thinking. If they are the latter develop new beliefs about yourself and consider how they might change your career path with your current or future employer.

46 TO CONVINCE OTHERS, YOU MUST FIRST CONVINCE YOURSELF

Bristol quotes a Dr Walter Dill Scott, saying that 'success or failure in business is caused more by mental attitudes than by mental capabilities.' Self-belief is the most important thing you have.

The Matrix is a film which neatly illustrates many of the points that Bristol makes in *The Magic of Believing*. In one scene Neo and Morpheus are kung-fu fighting in a simulated training environment whilst still hooked up to the device that implants them inside the matrix. In other words, they are not physically fighting, but are sparring inside their heads. Having been programmed to kung-fu fight, Neo is challenged by Morpheus to show him how good he is. As they fight it out, Neo never quite gets to the point where is able to beat his mentor. Morpheus stops Neo and quizzes him as to why he cannot beat him and after a brief exchange challenges him with the words, 'You're faster than this… Don't think you are, know you are.' In essence he is telling Neo that he needs to convince himself that he is able to beat him before he actually can. After this, they resume the fight and Neo defeats Morpheus. Having done this Morpheus loads the 'jump program' in which Neo is expected to jump across two buildings some distance apart. Having watched Morpheus successfully land on the other building, Neo attempts to convince himself that he too can make what is a seemingly impossible jump. Unfortunately, he is clearly not convincing enough as he falls to the ground. As the film goes on Neo finally gets to the point where he does believe in himself and ultimately defeats the Matrix.

Although Bristol wrote his book decades earlier, he knew that in order to convince others, you had to first convince yourself. This is true in many other areas of life, particularly sports, where mental preparation is considered to be as important as physical ability. Olympic teams now employ a sports psychologist who works with the athletes to prepare for the games and help them believe that they have what it takes to win the gold medal. Bristol provides a great example of why it is so important to be convinced that you will succeed: 'It has long been my observation that a person with a workable idea seldom has any difficulty in getting money to finance himself. However, he must be thoroughly 'sold' on the idea himself before he can convince others to lend him money.'

In the end, if you don't believe in yourself, no one else will.

DEFINING IDEA...

'I figured that if I said it enough, I would convince the world that I really was the greatest.'

MUHAMMAD ALI

HERE'S AN IDEA FOR YOU...

The next time you have an idea to sell at work think about whether you are really convinced by it. Consider the counter arguments and the pitfalls associated with achieving it and if, after you have analyzed this you still believe in it, then it is highly likely that you will be able to convince others, no matter how sceptical they might be.

47 EVERYTHING CAN BE IMPROVED

'Bear in mind that no matter how long a piece of work has been done in a certain way, there's always a better way.' Throughout *The Magic of Believing*, Bristol entreats his readers always to question their daily lives and to rethink the way they do things.

When Bristol first published his book, the ravages of the Second World War were still fresh in America's memory. A generation of young men had returned to their families, forever changed by what they had endured. The homes they returned to had changed too. In their absence Americans had been forced to take on the home duties of a country at war. Productivity and innovation were the bywords of the day, as the war became the catalyst for efficiency and improvement.

In the post-war period people couldn't just go back. Normal routine had been irreversibly altered and a new standard had been set. The country had woken up to what could be achieved with the right attitude and the right impetus. If so much could be achieved during conflict, just think what the potential for peacetime could be! As a result, new industries evolved and technology advanced dramatically. Self-improvement blossomed as people re-evaluated their lives, with minds open to the possibilities of unlimited improvement. It was into this environment that Bristol launched his philosophies for living and readers were ready to hear the simple wisdom he espoused. *The Magic of Believing* is a book very much of its time in this sense, yet its ideas remain strikingly relevant today.

All that Bristol is asking of us is that we consider alternatives to our routines. There's not a moment to lose on the projects of our own lives. We need to wake up to this urgency and recognize that innovators are the ones who get ahead. To be innovators we have to start by voluntarily knocking ourselves off track in order to inspire new ideas, new ways of thinking.

This is not a new idea really. How many times have you been told to 'think outside the box'? The central message of this cliché remains pertinent. The 'blue sky thinking' beloved of the business world means leaving our comfort zones and going beyond the limits set by our predecessors. Rather than making do with how things are or sitting back and waiting for things to get better on their own, we should take the initiative in all situations. We should go about our lives with the certainty that there is nothing that cannot be improved.

Even better, we will cultivate the sort of creative mind from which new ideas naturally spring forth; the lightening bolt that hits us as if out of the blue and leads to radical new solutions to age-old problems. By developing a questioning mind that continually seeks new ways around challenges and cultivating a sense of urgency to push us forward, the fertile power of the subconscious will bloom with new ideas to help us on our way.

DEFINING IDEA...

'There's always a better way. Find it!'

THOMAS A. EDISON

HERE'S AN IDEA FOR YOU...

Question every process or activity in your home and work life – are you really following convention because it's the best way? When starting a new project put aside the accepted ways and try brainstorming improvements with your coworkers. Chances are there will be processes that can be improved upon. Senior management are bound to appreciate the enthusiasm this generates within your department.

48 MANTRAS AND SELF-AFFIRMATIONS

Retraining your mind is easier than you think.

As Bristol developed his ideas he spent a lot of time studying religions and cults. His research led him to believe that the success of both mainstream religions as well as obscure cults relied heavily on the repetition of chants, incantations, litanies and mantras. Repeating these daily, and sometimes more often, formed the basis for immersion, even indoctrination, in the religion or cult concerned. Looking at this objectively, Bristol could see the value that such techniques could bring and believed they had a place in making beliefs real and achievable. Indeed, he used a form of repetition when he first started in investment banking. Although lowly paid to begin with, he constantly doodled as he worked; always the dollar sign, and always more than one. Over time he accumulated more dollars as his career in investment banking advanced.

It is well known that the mind cannot tell the difference between the real world and the dream world. Just recall a dream you had in the past; at the time it probably seemed very real even though you were asleep. If the mind can create vivid dreams out of your subconscious, Bristol's observations regarding mantras and incantations seem highly plausible.

Many neurolinguistic programming (NLP) courses end with a rite of passage, designed to signify a new 'powerful' you. Those run by Anthony Robbins (one of the greatest proponents of NLP) require that you walk barefoot across hot coals; another involves breaking an arrow on your neck. The arrow has a wooded shaft and metal point, so could easily do serious damage to those taking part. Preparation is everything and key to this is the use of mantras designed to prepare the participants mentally for the challenge ahead. Given the need to be strong and powerful the mantras are suitably framed so that everyone believes they are strong enough to break the arrow. As, one by one, the participants succeed in the task it is clear that this is an exhilarating experience which illustrates just how powerful the mind can be. The reason why this works so well is down to something called Hebbian Learning. Once neurons have fired together more than once, the cells and synapses between them change chemically so that when one neuron fires it will be a stronger trigger to the other. So, the more you repeat the mantra, the stronger it becomes and the more likely it is that your brain will believe it.

DEFINING IDEA...

'One comes to believe whatever one repeats to oneself sufficiently often, whether the statement be true or false. It comes to be dominating thought in one's mind.'

ROBERT COLLIER, SLEF-HELP AUTHOR

HERE'S AN IDEA FOR YOU ...

Think about how you want to portray yourself: perhaps, for example, you want to appear confident. Whatever, it might be, develop a suitable mantra. Repeat it a few times each day and it won't be long before your brain will believe it.

49 THE PLACEBO EFFECT

Sometimes the dream world appears to be more real than the real world.

Bristol speaks at length on how the imagination, or what he also terms 'picture-making', can have quite surprising results, especially in the way the imagination can seemingly trick the mind. He provides plenty of examples where the imagination has overridden the conscious mind.

Margaretta West was returning on a troop ship from the South Pacific and found herself packed into a cabin with 17 other women. The cabin was airless and stifling and the portholes were shut and blackened so that no light could get out (it was wartime after all). As they happened to be in port, the captain permitted portholes to be opened after lights out. Margaretta decided that they had to get some air so opened the portholes to allow everyone to get some sleep. When they awoke the next morning, after sleeping soundly, they found that Margaretta had only opened the inner of the two portholes; the outer ones were still firmly shut and blackened out. So, although they thought they were getting fresh air and some respite from the heat, it was all in the mind.

Effects such as this are well known and are used in medicine, by mentalists and magicians and very often employed by expert sales people. The placebo effect in medicine is particularly powerful given that patients taking inert drugs display the same physiological reactions as those taking the real ones. It is believed that when people already know what the result of taking a pill is supposed to be, they unconsciously change their reaction to the drug to bring about the expected result.

They also report the result even if the actual outcome was different. In simple terms they become conditioned in the same way Pavlov was able to condition his dog to salivate at the sound of a ringing bell.

Bristol is careful to stress that harnessing your imagination is about more than just daydreaming. He believes that daydreaming, or undirected wishful thinking as he called it, will never release the internal forces that allow you to realize your goals. Instead, you have to actively cultivate the mental image, play it out and enhance it until it appears very real and more importantly, realizable. Perhaps one of the reasons why the placebo effect is so powerful is that people believe in the outcome so strongly that it makes any other outcome impossible.

DEFINING IDEA…

'Have you ever had a dream, Neo, that you were so sure was real? What if you were unable to wake from that dream, Neo? How would you know the difference between the dream world and the real world?'

MORPHEUS IN THE MATRIX

HERE'S AN IDEA FOR YOU…

Once you have set yourself a goal – it might be receiving an award at work, or buying the house of your dreams, for example – think about how you can make it real by imagining it first. Develop a well thought out image. If it is detailed enough, your brain will perceive it to be real

50 THE WHOLE PACKAGE

As any marketing executive will tell you, packaging is important. For us, says Bristol, that means 'the world accepts you as you appear to be.' If you look successful, people will assume you are.

Television shows such as *Ten Years Younger* and *How to look good naked* are all designed to give women confidence in their own bodies and the clothes that they wear. In *Ten Years Younger* the presenter takes a woman onto the high street and asks the general public to say how old they think she is. In most cases the average age from the general public's point of view is up to 15 years older than the participant's actual age. This acts as a spur for the woman to think about her image and the way she dresses. Once the transformation is complete, the public viewing is repeated and in all cases, the woman's age comes down to at least their actual age, if not quite a bit below.

Such shows demonstrate the importance we place on how people look and what they wear. It is well known that physical attractiveness is a significant factor in someone's success and there have been plenty of studies that have highlighted how looks can affect behaviour. Consider the following: neonatal nurses spend more time with healthy infants with normal birth weights than they do with other babies; parents give more attention to their most attractive children who as a result tend to be more balanced and socially skilled than their less attractive offspring; teachers expect good looking children to do better than those of average looks; and the more attractive amongst us tend to earn more and have better career chances. It seems that such things are a fact of life and we have been conditioned through our evolutionary roots to make judgements about other people based upon their looks and physical attractiveness.

Bristol was acutely aware of the importance of what he termed 'packaging' and asked his readers to consider whether they had eye-appeal and an appearance that set them apart from the crowd. He suggested that we take the lead from the automobile companies and Hollywood make-up artists, who know the value of eye-appeal, and believed that when you have a combination of proper packaging and highest quality goods within, you have an unbeatable combination. From his point of view, 'If you are properly attired when you are starting out on some important undertaking, you feel within yourself that sense of power, which will cause people to give way before you and will even stir others to help you on your way.' It is true. If you wear an expensive shirt, suit and tie you feel better, more successful and invincible. It's rather like putting on a suit of armour: it changes your self-perception and the perception formed by those around you.

DEFINING IDEA...

'The world sums you up by the clothes that you wear, and treats you accordingly.'

AL KORAN, BRITISH MENTALIST

HERE'S AN IDEA FOR YOU...

Have you given much thought to how you look and what you wear? Think about the clothes you wear and how they make you feel. What do they tell the world about you? Consider how you want to be perceived and aim to dress accordingly.

51 SET THE SCENE FOR SUCCESS

'Various lighting arrangements, different paraphernalia, often a special garb for those directing the operations, all to the accompaniment of soft, often religious music help to create a mystical atmosphere in order to put you in the proper emotional, and incidentally receptive, state.' So Bristol describes the various props and tactics used by religions and orders of all sorts to create the desired effect in their followers.

He isn't having a go at religion for the sake of it. In fact he goes on to provide other examples as variations on the same theme. His point is to highlight the great lengths to which people have always gone to create the sort of atmosphere that aids the cultivation of belief. Step into a place of worship, like the beautiful St Paul's Cathedral in central London, and you are immediately impressed by a sense of majesty and reverence. The profound silence of the setting can be quite humbling and this is no accident. The devout would point to the presence of God, but the lighting, scene and aroma of the place certainly play a part too.

This is a basic truth – our surroundings affect our minds. A disorganized, messy room will cause our minds to feel cluttered too. The vibrations of the environment somehow resonate within us. This can affect our mood: we feel oppressed or limited by what we see around us. Conversely a wide, cloudless sky that stretches to the very edges of the horizon can open up our minds and give us a sublime sense of spaciousness and wonder. What happens naturally can be helped along by the scene we set for ourselves.

An ordered working environment will be conducive to a businesslike frame of mind. On the other hand a more casual ambience might unleash you inner tortured artist, although the jury's still out on this one.

The same is true of talismans and lucky charms (see Idea 7). More people than you might think carry them and consider them powerful objects. We might scoff at such things and think ourselves above it, but what about that lucky pair of socks – the ones with a proven track record of granting us the mystical power to succeed on numerous occasions? We joke about it among friends, but we make sure we wear them to that important interview, just in case. Similarly, as Bristol says, 'a cracked or broken mirror isn't going to bring you bad luck unless you believe in it.'

Legendary varsity American football coach, Erk Russell convinced his team, the Georgia Southern College Eagles, that a muddy ditch at the bottom of the field was none other than 'Beautiful Eagle Creek', the source of 'magical waters'. All the team had to do was anoint the away-team's field with the water, carried in a jug to every game, and its magical properties would see them right. Sure enough, the team went on to win many championships and the jug is displayed proudly to this day as a powerful symbol of victory.

DEFINING IDEA...
'Outer order contributes to inner calm.'
GRETCHEN RUBIN, THE HAPPINESS PROJECT

HERE'S AN IDEA FOR YOU...
If you're a naturally untidy person try employing the mantra 'a place for everything and everything in its place' when dealing with your work space. Spending a morning tidying your inbox or filing away papers may feel like a waste of time, but when you next sit down to work, your decluttered desk will free your mind from distractions and set it in the mood to work productively on the task at hand.

52 THE SINGULARITY

Self-belief is crucial, but following through and persistence are just as important.

According to Bristol, belief is the motivating force that enables you to achieve your goal. It's true that without the belief that something is worth doing it is highly unlikely that you will ever get off your sofa and achieve it. That doesn't mean that belief is all you need however, as success also requires hard work and persistence, especially when you are faced with obstacles. Holding onto the belief for as long as it takes to achieve your goals may be termed the 'singularity'.

To be truly successful requires the self-belief and focus of someone like Johan Harmenberg. Born in Stockholm in 1954, Harmenberg took up fencing at the tender age of 11 and went on to win the individual men's épée at the 1980 Moscow Olympic games. Although winning Olympic Gold is an amazing achievement in its own right, what is even more amazing is how he got there, since in doing so he fundamentally changed the nature of Olympic épée fencing. As Harmenberg stated in his book, *Epee 2.0*, classic fencing had always assumed that the fencer with the superior technique would always control the outcome; that the one who maintained the longer distance had the advantage and that the key to victory lay in defeating the opponent's best moves. Having given up competitive fencing because he believed he lacked the talent to fence classically, Harmenberg started to experiment with his coach's belief that this received wisdom could be completely overturned (having mapped out the new paradigm on a napkin). His ideas and skills were initially met with derision and despite being a highly competent fencer he was snubbed by the Swedish selection committee. This did not deter him and led him to one conclusion – either he stopped fencing for good or he would win the 1980 Individual Epée Olympic Gold Medal. Embarking on a two year campaign, where nothing but fencing consumed his life, he went on to win the gold using techniques that everyone thought would lead to failure. Harmenberg's singularity was the self-belief in his épée 2.0 paradigm and the singular focus on winning the Gold Medal.

DEFINING IDEA...

'Take up one idea. Make that one idea your life – think of it, dream of it, live on that idea. Let the brain, muscles, nerves, every part of your body, be full of that idea, and just leave every other idea alone. This is the way to success.'

SWAMI VIVEKANANDA, HINDU MONK

HERE'S AN IDEA FOR YOU...

If there is something you really want to strive for, consider what it will take to reach it. Do you have the self-belief, tenacity and motivation to achieve it? Before you commit to it, write down what it will require of you, what obstacles you might face and what resources you may need. This will help to define your plan of action and more importantly help you remain focused.

Printed in Great Britain
by Amazon